To Owen Luder

With many th___ ___ ___ ___ lifetime
of ___ ___ architects and ___ the ABS

Signature

1/12/05

SPECIAL HOUSES FOR SPECIAL PEOPLE

SPECIAL HOUSES FOR SPECIAL PEOPLE

by

Brian Lingard DA (Manc) FRIBA

First published in 2005 by
The Memoir Club
Stanhope Old Hall
Stanhope
Weardale
County Durham

British Library Cataloguing in
Publication Data.
A catalogue record for this book
is available from the
British Library

ISBN: 1-84104-129-7

Typeset by Lintons Printers, Crook, Co. Durham
Printed by CPI Bath

To my wife Dorothy
and
Christopher
Timothy
Rebecca
Debbie
Jane
Cordelia
Emily
and
Charles

Special Houses for Special People

Contents

Chapters

Brian Lingard began his architectural studies in Manchester during the war years, but those studies were interrupted by service in the Royal Navy towards the end of the war. Victory in Europe day on 8 May 1945 was spent swinging on an anchor out in Gibraltar harbour, his ship, HMS *Wolverine*, having drawn the short straw of being duty destroyer for the port on that day, with all shore leave suspended, resulting in a consequent frustrating absence from the celebrations raging ashore!

Subsequent days were spent going out into the seas around Gibraltar to pick up U-boats, which were popping up to surrender, and then escorting a convoy of these submarines up to the River Foyle in Northern Ireland where they were being gathered together prior to being taken out into the Atlantic for scuttling to their graveyard in the depths of the ocean.

Victory over Japan followed a few months later and then, eventually, demobilization, with a return to architectural studies possible in 1947.

Associateship of the RIBA was achieved in 1949 and, with Diploma examinations concluded in the early summer of that year, Diploma day was on 16 July. Dorothy, Brian's fiancée, studying drama at the nearby Royal Northern College of Music, finished her last term on the same day. Dorothy and Brian married four days later on 20 July 1949.

With imminent marriage in view, the need for a salaried job for Brian was an immediate and, indeed, urgent necessity. Job interviews in mid-1949 produced offers from public authority architectural offices (there was little work on offer in private practice in these immediate post-war years) at salaries ranging from £420 to £450 per annum. A post for a higher grade of £480 per annum was advertised by the Anglesey County Council and, with memories of idyllic childhood holidays in West Wales, Dorothy and Brian thought that this might be an ideal starting point for salaried architectural status.

Two visits to Anglesey followed, the first on a hot, sunny day in May for the job interview, an offer of the post being received on the spot. The second visit was to inspect a possible first home; tucked away on the outskirts of a village in the middle of the island, Hafod Newydd (circa 1850) was a one-time farmhouse surrounded by 50 acres of its own farmland, furnished, but without running water, electricity or any other services - nevertheless all available for £2 weekly. Job and home settled, Dorothy and Brian embarked upon their new life in Anglesey in those last days of July 1949, without pause for an extended honeymoon.

Nine months of work in a local authority department was then sufficient to convince Brian Lingard that work in an architectural office headed by someone else, particularly in a bureaucratic environment, was not for him. The beginnings of the rest of the story are encapsulated in subsequent pages.

Rhydysbardyn interior

The first 'new' house illustrated is not really part of the family of special new houses for special people which is the subject of this book but, without it, perhaps none of the houses which follow would have been built.

When first coming to Anglesey, Dorothy and I occupied a farmhouse on the edge of a village in the centre of the island. We got to know our farmer neighbours, who lived a few hundred yards away down the lane and over the hill, because Mrs Hughes, as was the custom in those days, reared the poultry of the farm. The memory of her ducks, plucked and ready for the oven, still make the gastric juices run. One evening we were invited over for supper and we arrived to find an enormous goose had been roasted in our honour, accompanied by an equally enormous bowl of carrots, pulled that day from a field on the farm and running with the yellow salted butter, churned from the milk of the homestead.

Hafod Newydd

During the course of the meal it was mentioned that we were looking for a house close to Llangefni, the county town, as a permanent home and Mr Hughes told us that he knew of a house for sale which might well suit us. Furthermore, if we decided to buy the house he would rent the 11 acres of grazing land which went with it for £40 a year.

Rhydysbardyn turned out to be a fine example of a traditional Welsh longhouse particularized by Iorwerth Peate in his book *The Welsh House*. It had been built in the early 18th century and had been a coaching inn on the old Menai Bridge/Holyhead road before the A5 was built across the island by Thomas Telford. John Wesley had preached there on his tour of North Wales in the late 18th century. The stone for the house had been quarried from the field in front of the dwelling and the resulting circular pit had been used as the local cock fighting arena until quite recent times. The '...sbardyn' in Rhydysbardyn was said to be either a reference to the spurs fixed to the legs of the fighting cocks or to the 'spurring' of the horses needed to mount the steep hill up the road to the house after crossing the stream which ran along the bottom boundary of the land.

We found the house to be occupied by an old lady who was asking £1,200 for the property. With mortgage interest rates at about 4.5% in those days it seemed that the rent for the land was almost going to pay that interest and the bargain was too good to resist. Another factor was that the Government had that year introduced the concept, for the first time, of Improvement Grants for equipping old houses which were without modern facilities with those facilities: up to 50% of a sum not exceeding £600.

Rhydysbardyn was built of stone with external walls which were three feet thick and the house had a roof of Welsh slate. It had neither electricity or gas, or mains water or any form of drainage. Furthermore there was no hope of any of these services arriving in the foreseeable future. Drinking water had to be carried in a bucket from a well by the stream at the bottom of the fields.

After guiding the local rural district council through the regulations for the new grants, of which at first they knew nothing, we obtained the first Improvement Grant in Anglesey (for £300) for Rhydysbardyn. Employing the Parry Brothers, a firm of local builders, we converted the cowhouse which formed an extension to the dwelling to make the new kitchen, dining and bathroom wing; a 500-gallon rainwater tank was provided to catch the rainwater from the roof, the water to be pumped up by hand each day to a small tank in the roof; a Wellstood solid fuel cooker, which never went out, was installed for cooking, heating the dining-kitchen and to provide the hot water; drains were dug, a septic tank was constructed; and piped calor gas lighting was installed throughout the ground floor.

Rhydysbardyn

Great care was taken not to disturb the external historic character of the dwelling. We built a new dormer window into the rear of the house roof to provide more light and headroom to the main bedroom and an enormous century-old bulge in the rear wall was propped up, but preserved, by means of a new massive stone buttress which we built to support the centre of the bulge. All this for £600, half of which had been provided by our local council.

The photographs show the open plan modern interior of this nearly three hundred year old dwelling; the exterior as it was at the time the builders started work; and the setting of the house as it still is today, little changed since the 18th century. Also shown is a photograph of our first rented home - Hafod Newydd.

One event concerning Rhydysbardyn stands out in my mind and this concerned the Coronation of Queen Elizabeth II. In 1953, the higher parts of Anglesey were just within reach of a television signal from the newly constructed Holme Moss transmitter a hundred miles away on the Lancashire/Yorkshire border. A television set could be purchased to receive that faint signal and thus enable us to see the Coronation on television, but it could not be powered by calor gas! The solution was a second-hand, petrol-driven electricity generator providing about a kilowatt of power at 230 volts, housed on the seat of the old, free-standing privy by the back door and wired back to the set in the sitting room.

Television thus came to Rhydysbardyn just in time for the Coronation, which was watched by a group of friends at the house on the day. The second-hand generator was not however as reliable as the previous owner had made it out to be and, after an hour or so of the ceremony, the picture suddenly disappeared into a white spot in the middle of the screen. Priming and cranking were needed to re-start the engine before the picture could be recovered and this routine turned out to be a regular feature of our television viewing over the next year or two.

The added hazard was a 5 foot 3 inch lintel height for the back door (the population of Anglesey tended to be rather small in the 18th century!) which was often forgotten in relation to my own 6 foot 2 inches in the rush to re-start the generator in the middle of a play, resulting in some nasty head wounds in the cause of family entertainment.

Left to right - Roberts house,
Thomas house

"O.C. NALGO and O.C. Cricket" was how Tony Thomas, the Weights and Measures Inspector of the Anglesey County Council introduced himself at our first meeting at those offices. The offer of membership of the former was declined politely, but I expressed enthusiasm for the possibility of being useful when he was wearing the other hat. We got to know each other well on the cricket field that summer, but there was a parting of the ways when I left the County Council for private practice the following year.

Our next meeting was late one afternoon when there was a heavy step on the bare timber staircase leading to my rear, single-room, ten shillings-a-week office in Llangefni. In came Tony Thomas bearing a drawing showing a small area of land edged in red which he had just agreed to purchase as the site for a new house for himself and his family in Menai Bridge. After a little skirmishing over the extent of the percentage fee, I was awarded my first commission for a brand new house.

In these immediate post-war years, all building work over £100 in value had to be licensed and licences for completely new houses were very few and far between. In this case, the fact that the land was owned by one of the local Councils, who had the responsibility for allocating licences, and that the purchaser was a senior officer of the County Council no doubt assisted in the award of the licence, but this was only the beginning of the licensing problem. No house could exceed 1,500 square feet; no more than a standard and a half of softwood could be used in the construction and the use of steel was limited to little more than was needed for the door and window lintels. The budget for the house was £2,500 and my fee within that budget was to be £130 for full architectural services to the completion of the building contract.

A single storey house was stipulated, having two living rooms and four bedrooms, to house the family of four, including two school-aged children.

An inspection of the site revealed quite a steep slope across the road frontage, posing the possibility of expensive work below floor level. The solution was a twin-gabled house with a split-level floor area divided by a flight of five or six steps between the living areas and the lower bedroom wing. Cedar shingles (unrationed) were used for the pitched roofs to lighten the loading and thus to eke out the timber ration. The house was built as licensed and within budget, resulting in a satisfied client and my return to the town cricket team for a few more seasons!

A year or two later, a commission was received to design and build a house on the adjoining plot for Mr Roberts, a widowed father, and his daughter. The site had remained undeveloped because of the increasing gradient of the slope of the ground above the Thomas house. The solution here was to build the garage at the lowest part of the site, with the single storey of living accommodation to the side of the garage, but with the house floor level at garage roof level and the approach to the front door up a flight of external steps and across the terrace formed by the flat garage roof.

The two houses are shown together on the photograph taken shortly after the construction of the second house. The circular stone gate piers marking the drive openings to the two houses were a traditional feature of the Anglesey countryside.

A deliberate decision has been taken not to include any floor plans in this not-too-technical book. There is a limit to the major variations which can occur in the disposition of domestic accommodation in modest dwellings and the emphasis has thus been rather upon the effect that the buildings have had on their environment and the community.

Idris Davies house

The second commission for a new private house also came from one of my former colleagues at the County Council. Idris Davies was a solicitor, the deputy Clerk to the Council, and had married recently. He had found a site in Menai Bridge slightly inland from the Menai Straits but on high ground commanding magnificent views to the south-east, with an uninterrupted prospect down to the Straits and to a 20-mile span of the highest peaks of Snowdonia beyond.

His two-storey house was to occupy the whole of the permitted 1,500 square feet and this made conforming to the timber and steel licence limits most difficult. By juggling the available timber against the permitted steel it was possible to reduce the depth of the timber first floor joists to about half the usual depth and, in that way, the house was built within the legal licence limits.

The building licence also stipulated the maximum sum which could be spent under the licensing terms. This was not a matter which could be ignored as the architect Raglan Squire found to his cost when he exceeded the licensed limit for his Transport Pavilion in the 1951 Festival of Britain Exhibition. In his 1984 auto-biography *Portrait of an Architect*, he recounts how he was charged with a criminal offence for exceeding the licensed limit on that building and had to face judge and jury in court to answer the charge. In the event he was exonerated on technical grounds, but many architects quivered at the time with a " ...there but for the grace of God go I" feeling waking them in the small hours of the night!

Another problem which affected the budget for new houses in the early 1950s was the Development Charge which had been introduced by the Attlee Government with the 1947 Town and Country Planning Act. This required anyone developing land with a new building for which they had received planning permission, to pay to the Government the whole of the difference between the value of the land with and without that planning permission. I recollect that this amounted to about £200 for this site, which represented a big slice of the £3,500 budget for the house.

The Development Charge disappeared later in the 1950s after the Conservatives had returned to office but, in this century it has, in effect, appeared once again with the Blair Government stipulation that a third or more of new houses built on sites for which planning permission is awarded should be 'affordable houses' at the expense of the landowner; all this in addition to the capital gains tax arising on the sale of building land.

The photograph of the house is a present day photograph taken some 50 years after completion of the first contract. A few years after completion of the original house I was commissioned to carry out alterations. With three young sons making the house seem rather small, there was a need for more living space and the integral garage was converted to form a further room for the house. A new canopy was designed for the front door and the garage was replaced by a free-standing structure. Otherwise however, the house remained in the first years of the new millenium in much the same form as originally designed and, over 50 years on, with Mr and Mrs Idris Davis still in occupation!

CLAPBOARDS AND LEADED LIGHTS

King house

Many Anglesey residents were sea-faring folk and the Kings were of that calling. Mr King was a merchant navy officer who lived with his wife in Llangefni, but spent most of each year sailing the oceans of the world. On their visit to my office he explained that he was home on leave and that, before the end of that leave in ten days' time, they wished to approve full design drawings and an agreed budget for their new home. Mr King would be returning in a few months' time to occupy the house on his next leave!

Their site was an infilling strip of land in the middle of a group of good quality, pre-war houses and it had been left undeveloped because the boundary on one side was a small stream from which the ground rose quite steeply to the other parallel boundary lying some 25 yards away.

A common feature of couples intent on having a house built specially for themselves is that they have spent several years collecting cuttings from magazines illustrating features which are a must for their own dwelling. The Kings were no exception to that rule and they came armed with copies of photographs of their ideal home from *Ideal Homes*, all of which demonstrated their intense enthusiasm for the Tudor period of domestic architecture.

My normal response to such an avalanche of cuttings was to listen attentively to what was being said, make careful notes and file the cuttings, but then endeavour to put forward design proposals which also were based firmly upon the accommodation requirements, on an honest use of local materials and the limitations or opportunities afforded by the site. In most cases, given time and patience, the design proposals would prevail but in this case, time was of the essence and compromise was inevitable.

The solution was the introduction of a timber-clad, half-height, first storey with dormer windows for the bedrooms - a typical feature of 16th century domestic architecture - and, for the first and last time in my professional career, the use of (genuine) lead cams to divide all the glazing into little diamond shapes. The house was designed to a narrow (cottage) width, tight up against the upper site boundary on the shallower part of the slope, leaving the remainder of the site frontage to form the garden, sloping down to the stream which ran along the lower boundary. White rendered walls and slated roofs completed the picture.

The design proposals and budget were accepted two days before Mr King rejoined his ship and the couple moved into their new house several months later on his return from a voyage to the Antipodes.

Dormer windows and leaded lights

John Williams house

John Williams was the Clerk to a rural district council and had found an acre of land within his Rural District on the main coastal road just a few hundred yards away from one of the best beaches on the island, on which to build a new house for his family. We had met on several occasions when planning applications were being lodged with his Council for passing on to the County Planning Office for their consideration. In the early 1950s small rural district councils were run by the Clerk and his secretary, supported by the Surveyor whose sole assistant would be a lad fresh from school to make the tea and to hold the end of a measuring tape.

The site was a fine one for a new house, but it was well away from other dwellings and the 1947 Town and Country Planning Act was strongly biased against awarding permissions for isolated new dwellings in the countryside. I have always felt that this has been one of the failures of our post-war planning system. Our countryside has been enriched over hundreds of years by the building of individual dwellings in positions which, with associated tree planting and good landscape integration, can contribute much to the balance of the rural environment.

Apart from cottages for farm workers, however, and the very occasional large mansion in extensive parkland, we have seen few such additions to the countryside. There are many small hamlets and villages which would benefit greatly from the construction of a well-designed, medium-sized dwelling standing in its own grounds just beyond the natural boundary of the settlement. There was a belated recognition of this problem by Central Government in early 1997 with the issue of a Planning Policy Guidance note on the subject, but planning authorities generally have remained adamant that single houses in the countryside should not be permitted and it is thus now over 60 years since we have seen any real continuation of this ancient tradition.

But back to the John Williams site. We did indeed have much opposition from the planning authority to this proposal for an isolated house in the countryside and there were two site planning sub-committee meetings before outline approval was obtained, no doubt with good support from the local members on the planning committee for their RDC Clerk, despite opposition from the planning officer.

I received many further commissions for new houses on the strength (it was said) of the attractive nature of this prominently placed house and it would therefore seem that, despite planner's reservations, the building of a house in this countryside position was regarded locally as being something of an asset to the environment rather than a detriment.

When giving consideration to the many examples of fine historic dwellings set in the open countryside, I was reminded that the 'bible' for students on architectural history was *The History of Architecture on the Comparative Method* by Sir Banister Fletcher. This 1,300 page epic, reprinted many times between first publication in 1896 and the latest edition in 1996, carried many meticulous and beautiful drawings of significant historic buildings of the world from those of the earliest civilizations to 1835, when historic architecture was deemed to have ceased by Sir Banister. This was also the case with the RIBA, who would not accept any building executed after that date as being suitable for measured Testimonies of Study by their students.

My favourite story concerning Banister Fletcher stems from the time when he was President of the RIBA and was receiving guests at a professional function. Amongst the architects arriving for the occasion was Edward Maufe, a generation younger than the President, not yet holding the status within the profession he was to acquire in later life. On his arrival, he felt it necessary to identify himself when approaching his President with outstretched hand:

'I'm Maufe', he announced.

Sir Banister seemed shocked.

'But you can't do that my dear chap, we're only just starting.'

Duncan house

Miss Duncan was a middle-aged lady who owned a bookshop on the Wirral. She floated into my office one morning, complete with twinset and pearls, with the news that she had purchased a smallholding high up on the slopes of Llaneillian 'mountain' at the northern tip of Anglesey. The cottage on those 20 or so acres of grazing land was occupied by a gnarled son-of-the soil who was to have a range of new pigsties to replace the tumbledown stone structures which presently housed the pig population of the holding.

After brushing up on the essential dimensions and character of the modern pigsty, I visited the site, prepared the appropriate drawings and handed over the completed pigsties to Miss Duncan a month or two later. This all turned out to be something of a test for the young architect because, after expressing satisfaction with the new piggery it was a case of '... now we can get on with my new house'.

The site chosen for the new house was kept up wind of, and at an appropriate distance away from, the swine but, unavoidably, that site sloped steeply down the mountainside, albeit commanding magnificent views of the coastline below and the Irish Sea beyond. The single storied-house which was stipulated was balanced out over a large stone-walled garage at the lower level to take up the steep slope across the site of the house. The views through the large windows positioned to capture their expanse were quite breathtaking. *Ideal Homes* carried a featured article of this house in 1954.

My client was well-informed and particular over details for the design and equipment of the house interior. I was reminded by these carefully detailed instructions of another similar lady client who directed me to ensure that the material for the lavatory seats should be non-scratchable as it was her experience that the metal suspenders supporting her stockings would cause irreparable damage to more vulnerable seat material. Imagination still boggles at the thought!

The approach elevation   *From the windows*

Miss Duncan was instrumental in my introduction to Sir John Lomax, the then UK Ambassador to Bolivia, who was shortly to retire and who had bought a house lower down the mountainside with that retirement in view. He wished to carry out some refurbishments and alterations to the house and I was asked to undertake that work.

One of the features of that commission was the installation of a new hardwood staircase to be built to outline measurements provided by myself but to be constructed with detailed carvings to be undertaken by a Spanish-speaking joiner in La Paz, the capital. This was not an easy liaison and I was much relieved when the staircase finally arrived safely in Liverpool by ship from South America. It was then installed in the house where intended, fortunately as an exact fit for the allocated space and height. The dark, polished, heavily-carved, tropical hardwood looked magnificent set against the white walls of the entrance hall of the old house.

When Sir John came to inspect the finished house, he told me of his audience with the Queen a few days earlier. It seems that he had told Her Majesty about the primitive conditions which still existed in Bolivia in the mid-20th century, in particular that the main shopping street in La Paz terminated abruptly after a few hundred yards at the edge of the jungle, which then extended for several hundred miles to the next point of civilization. The Queen ventured the view that it must be very difficult for most of the population of Bolivia to live without the benefit of mains water, drainage and electricity for their everyday needs. Sir John told me that he responded, rather apologetically, to say that he was in fact retiring to a part of Her Majesty's realm, only some 300 miles from London, where he also was not going to be able to enjoy the benefits of mains water, main drainage or electricity!

DOCTORS IN LOVE

Dr Jones house

Of the many friends Dorothy and I made in Anglesey during our years on the island, almost half were members of the medical profession. GPs in Anglesey and hospital consultants from the Bangor hospitals figured prominently in that circle of friends and many of them became clients.

The difficulty in maintaining friendships with doctors in private practice in Anglesey in those days was that they were often sole practitioners or, at best, the junior doctor in a two-doctor partnership. They were thus perpetually on call and an evening out at a local restaurant was very often disturbed by an urgent telephone call which meant that one of our party of four would be absent between the soup and the coffee tending to the last rites of one of the local population or supervising the white line walking of over-indulgent motorists holed up in the police station.

I was commissioned by two Anglesey doctors who became the Drs Jones, Brynsiencyn. He was the local GP and his future wife was a doctor on the staff of the County Council. They were both extremely busy people and briefing sessions were restricted to gaps between surgeries when the lady of the imminent marriage was also able to snatch an hour away from her community duties.

The site was a magnificent one, lying towards the southern end of the Menai Straits on the edge of the village of Brynsiencyn and commanding a wider view of the Straits as far as the open sea and of the Caernarfonshire mountains than was available from the Menai Bridge area. The site contained the stone foundations of an earlier building and the house was designed to take advantage of that existing structure. Part two-storey and part single-storey, the roof of the single-storey section was laid out as a terrace to serve the first floor bedrooms, overlooking the fine views southwards from the house.

Detailed planning permission for the proposed design was obtained without difficulty from the planning authority, traditional rendered brickwork walls being used for the external wall surfaces of the building. The main 300 mm thick walls of the structure were taken through to be expressed beyond the general wall surfaces and some heightened contrast was needed between these different surfaces.

I had previously observed that the traditional rendering of domestic structures in Anglesey could be 'coloured' in two ways. The first of these was by the use of limewash which whitened the surface of the rendering. This was always applied to the walls, and sometimes also to the roof, of the farm buildings attached to the farmhouses, but rarely to the houses themselves. I recall suggesting to one farmer that the whitening should be carried on over the house as well as the buildings, but he was insistent that the house should not be treated in that way. His reason was that the limewashing on the farm buildings was applied as an antiseptic and not for decoration. It was important to ensure that the house was seen as being where the family lived and not the animals.

The second form of treatment for external rendered surfaces was to use the red impregnated soils of Parys Mountain in the north of the island (where copper, lead and silver had been mined since Roman times) as a solution in water to form a colouring matrix for application to the external walls of cottages. The result was a strong rusty red appearance for the walls. The practice had died away in recent years but there were some instances of this usage still evident in parts of the island.

The approach from the north

The hall

The south-west elevation and terraces

I decided to use these contrasting white and rusty red colours to define the structural elements of the load-bearing walls on the Drs Jones' house and this was well received by the clients. It was not however, well received by the planning officer who expressed his dismay at this stark contrast which had been created in such a visually exposed position. He asked that the external walls be re-painted to ensure that the house became white all over. I remonstrated by insisting that I had merely followed an old Anglesey tradition in the choice of colouring and referred to several places where the use of the Parys Mountain ochres could still be seen. I heard nothing more on that subject and the house (although subsequently extended by others) still carries that characteristic contrast in external colouring. I did not however endeavour to re-use the rusty red colouring for external walls again in Anglesey houses.

The house was featured with an illustrated article in the magazine *Homes and Gardens* and subsequently included (in what might be said to have been post-war sequel to *The Modern House in England* by F R S Yorke) in a book published by *Country Life* called *New Houses for Moderate Means* (1957) by H Dalton Clifford.

The house in the landscape

Our contractors for this house were the Parry Brothers of Llangefni, a well-established firm of builders with a strong local connection. The brothers Parry were used to conducting almost all of their everyday business in the Welsh language of their hearth. They were not comfortable when conversing in English with customers, even though the vocabulary of Wales is a little short on technical terms, which means that a conversation conducted in Welsh on building matters is peppered with English technical expressions.

Our best remembered encounter with the Parry Brothers occurred after the completion of the Rhydysbardyn contract and our occupation of that house. The first full summer in the house was a very dry one. The water in the rainwater storage tank was getting dangerously low and, with towelling nappies now requiring regular attention, apart from other needs, we considered how to supplement the rainwater supplies. We remembered that the Parry Brothers had brought up the water for our building works in a tank on the back of a lorry, so Dorothy telephoned to ask if they would let us have 500 gallons of water that day. John Parry took the call and there was a long silence at his end of the telephone. The subsequent conversation went something like this:-

Dorothy:	Are you still there Mr Parry?
John Parry:	Yes, indeed I am Mrs Lingard.
Dorothy:	Well, can you get it for me?
John Parry:	Diawl, I'm not sure that I can.
Dorothy (with rising irritation):	Why not Mr Parry - I am getting desperate over the washing.
John Parry:	How is that Mrs Lingard?
Dorothy:	Well, I must have water to wash the nappies.
John Parry:	Oh, there's <u>watter</u> it is you want. I thought you said mortar and I could not for the life of me think where I would get 500 gallons of mortar at such short notice!

The 500 gallons of H_2O arrived later that day.

The granary and the mill

The Williams family of Parciau, in the centre of the island, was one of the landowning families of Anglesey. Sir Lawrence Williams was the baronet in the 1950s and one of his major interests was his cricket field at Parciau and his sponsorship of the Parciau cricket team. It was said that one Sandy McNab arrived there on a summer's day to play cricket and remained to become a permanent resident at Parciau on the strength of his performance at, and round, the wicket! This amusing story of the Parciau set can be read in a book entitled *Across the Straits* written by Kyffin Williams, the eminent Royal Academician, who, when turning out for the Portmadog cricket team, played a number of fixtures at Parciau.

The eldest son, Francis Williams was a barrister, a distinguished wartime wing commander and the Birkenhead Recorder, who lived with his wife and four daughters in a fine historic manor house in Denbighshire. For weekend and holiday use, near to, but separate from, the family seat at Parciau, Francis Williams obtained a property in Talwrn consisting of a miller's house, a stone windmill shell and an associated granary. I was commissioned over a period of two or three years to convert and/or renovate all three buildings for the family and the first of these commissions, illustrated here, was the conversion of the granary.

The three floor levels within the granary were retained unaltered for domestic use. At the lower, entrance, level were the kitchen and dining areas; at the mezzanine level was the sitting area and at the upper level, over the entrance floor, were the bedroom and bathroom. The walls of the granary were 500 mm thick, solid stone walls, and such stone walls are far from weatherproof. This was achieved by lining the inside face of the external walls with a corrugated bitumen-impregnated vertical damproof membrane. The inside faces of the corrugated lathing were then plastered, leaving both an air cavity and an impregnable vertical dpc in the core of the composite wall. This was a detail of construction which proved to be invaluable over the years in Anglesey, making it possible to convert otherwise damp and cold rubble stone buildings into insulated and weatherproof domestic environments.

Split level living

The granary was used by the Williams family for many years until Lawrence Williams passed on to the great cricket field in the sky and Francis became Sir Francis and moved along the Anglesey lanes to Parciau for their family visits to the island.

James house

In the late 1930s my family took a house in Treaddur Bay in Anglesey for our annual fortnight-long summer holiday, a routine inherited from the previous generation when my grandfather and his young family would motor over from Cheshire to Anglesey for a similar holiday at the home of a Holyhead sea captain on the Dublin packet. In those early 20th century days this road journey was a hazardous undertaking, bearing in mind the unreliability of motor cars in those Sunbeam motoring days and the mountainous single track roads which were a feature of the Caernarfonshire stretches of the journey.

Our holiday house was a few yards down the road from the sea captain's home and was occupied, other than in the high summer months, by a family called James. From late July to early September the James's retreated into a shed in the back garden, leaving the house completely free for the use of the incoming holiday family. I can pinpoint the date of this holiday to late August 1937 because I recollect being allowed to get up at two o'clock in the morning of 31 August to listen, on the radio, to a rather crackly commentary from America on the Tommy Farr/Joe Louis heavyweight championship of the world boxing match at Madison Square Gardens - which went to fifteen rounds and ended in a narrow (much disputed) defeat on points for the British champion.

During the early 1950s I was approached by a young man, just married, who held a local government post and who wished to build a modestly priced bungalow on a plot of land he intended to purchase in Treaddur Bay. He told me that his name was James; not an uncommon name in Wales, but this evoked memories of the Treaddur Bay holiday of nearly twenty years previously. The plot of land turned out to be just a few hundred yards or so away from our holiday home and Mr James to be the nephew of our 1937 holiday hosts.

Although built for a modest sum this house was constructed using traditional materials, incorporating local stone features and with a generous frontage spread for a house on a limited budget.

Police house and station

Valley Police Station was a commission from the Anglesey County Council. It was essentially a small three-bedroomed house with an office attached, the house for the village policeman and his family on the main A5 road through the village. Oh for the days when every village had a resident policeman!

There is little that can be said about this small building project, other than it was welcome work for an embryonic architectural practice. One of the problems of the postwar profession has been that newly-qualified architects have had few opportunities for taking responsibility for a project right through from the brief for a new building to the issue of the final certificate. With the passing of the old pupilage system in the first part of the century - a system in which the pupil would actually pay the architect master a substantial sum for being a junior assistant in his office for five years whilst learning his profession - most architects were trained in schools of architecture and had little contact with the building industry until they emerged from the schools after a five-year, full-time course as fully fledged Associates of the Royal Institute of British Architects.

Usually, they then went into the vast architectural offices of a local authority, Government department or large private practice where they would, in effect, spend the next five years learning the practicalities of getting a building detailed and constructed - skills which had not been central to their studies in the schools of architecture. The difference with the old pupilage system was that they were now paid a salary and thus had to earn their keep whilst the learning process continued. That learning process in large offices however, invariably was conducted drawing obscure details for small parts of large buildings without ever seeing a project through from start to finish and many gaps were thus still left in their architectural education until early middle age.

In the old days, the pupil in a private practice office of probably no more than four or five people would soon find himself preparing all the drawings for a small scheme such as the Valley Police Station and then, under the direct eagle eye of the principal of the firm, attend site meetings and deal with most of the post-contract documentation for the building contract. He would be able to observe the construction of the building on a trade by trade basis from the digging of the foundations to the last coat of paint.

In the postwar years many architects never carried that complete responsibility for a new building until quite late in their careers and this resulted in many defects occurring in large building structures through lack of experience of the assistant architect with smaller projects on which they would have been intimately involved throughout the building process. Would that all architects could have had the experience of being directly responsible for several years at the outset of their careers for the small new buildings, domestic extensions and conversions which formed the grist of the work of a small private practice, before moving on to the detailing of larger and more complex structures. If the inevitable mistakes through lack of practical experience were to be made, far better that they were made as inexpensive, easily-remedied matters on small projects rather than resulting in extensive leakages over large areas of roof or window or in rampant condensation within a new major structure, as has so often occurred with major modern buildings.

In recent years, the schools of architecture have introduced years-out of college systems, with the period of training being extended to seven years before qualification, to ensure that the newly-qualified architect has had some practical office and site experience before being launched onto the public as a fully trained architect. However, that experience will more often than not have occurred in a large impersonal office rather than in a small private practice and much of this problem thus still remains for the profession.

The photograph of the police station is as it appears at the present day, with new windows and rendering, but the essential form and structure of the original building remains intact.

Wadsworth house

Modern architecture was slow to arrive in Britain in the 1930s. A student of architecture in that decade had little to see on the ground in the way of domestic architecture which corresponded to the work of the European icons who were the subject of his design studies. The immigration of architects from Europe such as Walter Gropius, Mies van der Rohe, Serge Chermayeff and Eric Mendelsohn hastened that arrival, but the building of new houses came to an abrupt halt in 1939 on the outbreak of war.

In the late 1940s therefore, newly qualified architects had gained their inspiration, not from built examples of modern architecture, but from architectural magazines and books such as *The Modern House in England* by F R S Yorke, *An Introduction to Modern Architecture* by J M Richards (1940), *Pioneers of the Modern Movement* by Nicholas Pevsner (1936) and, in particular, the *Oeuvre Complète* of Le Corbusier (which had run to four volumes by 1950) and his other publications.

Le Corbusier with his Villa Savoye at Poissy (1930) and his Pavilion Suisse in Paris, (1932) had a great influence on students of architecture in the pre- and immediate postwar years although, from my personal point of view, the construction of his Unité d'Habitation (1952) and the Chapel at Ronchamp (1955) marked a disappointing departure from the human scale and purity of his earlier work. One particular example of that earlier work which made a strong impression on me was a study for a small cottage described in the *Oeuvre Complète* as 'coté forèt, coté océan' - a *maison de vaçances*. The simple rhythm of that framed structure was much in my mind when designing an entry, in the late 1940s, for the annual student competition of the Manchester Society of Architects. The design was for a sailing club, which entry, rather surprisingly, was awarded the second prize.

Corbusier maison de vacances

View to the shore

Mrs Wadsworth, since pre-war days, had owned a small plot of land within a group of four or five houses on the southern coast road of Anglesey, immediately overlooking a fine small sandy bay (l'océan) hemmed in by rocky headlands on either side. The client had a tiny £1,000 budget for the construction of a holiday cottage to be used only in the summer months - a *maison de vaçances*.

The solution for this cottage was the construction of two massive side walls built in local random rubble stonework, with timber-framed front and rear walls and a low pitched felted roof slung between those stone walls. Facing south towards the sea, the external wall is mostly window, with non-window areas of the wall clad in waney-edged creosoted elm weather-boarding.

Although differing in structural character from the Corbusier *maison de vaçances*, the Wadsworth house was much influenced by that concept as the scale, usage and positioning of the two dwellings had so many coincidental affinities.

A gaffe occured on my part when, as the house neared occupation time, my client asked what I thought it should be called. Proud of my recently acquired few words of Welsh, off the cuff, I ventured that Ty Carreg Bach (little stone house) might be a suitable name. This was well received by the client but, when a different name was eventually chosen I was told that the reason was that it had been discovered that Ty Carreg Bach was the name given, in country areas of Wales, to the outdoor privy, usually built in stone separately from, and to the rear of, the bigger house!

JONES THE BUTCHERS

Lionel Jones house

Amongst the most interesting one-off house commissions were those from local tradesmen or businessmen: the lifeblood of the local economy, hard working, thrifty individuals whose aims in life often included being able to afford a specially built new house for their family.

The Jones were a long-established family of butchers in Llangefni. Father Jones, in retirement, handed on a series of thriving businesses to his three sons, Glyn, Lionel and Donald. Although meat was still rationed (until 1954) when Dorothy and I came to live in Anglesey, we were well looked after by the family, living as we were in the heart of this Welsh Black steer-raising and early Spring lamb county.

Butcher Glyn, who ran the main High Street shop of the family, already had a fairly modern bungalow on the outskirts of the town and he was a fanatic boxing fan. One day he asked me to visit his house to look at a problem which had arisen. I arrived, to be shown through the house and out of the back door to a large wooden building which occupied a great deal of the back garden. Inside was a boxing ring and a mass of boxing memorabilia decorating the walls and shelving around the ring. There was also a bad smell!

Glyn showed me a corner of the wooden floor under the lino covering which he had exposed and taken up that day and from where the bad smell was emanating. Looking below the floor boards with a torch (and a handkerchief applied to the nose) I could see wonderful areas of colourful fungus flowering out of the underside of the floor timbers. The flooring was riddled with dry rot due, I explained to Jones the Boxer, to the fact that there was no ventilation to the underfloor area and there was an air-tight seal to the timbers formed by the lino covering over the floor boards. There was nothing for it but a complete removal of the timber floor, linoleum and all, then treatment of the underfloor walls and concrete and the complete replacement of the timbers, this time well-ventilated.

Butcher Lionel had his shop on Church Street, round the corner from Glyn's shop. He was essentially the pork butchering side of the family, but their products overlapped in many ways and Lionel also specialised in mutton (as distinct from lamb) which was still regarded as a delicacy on the island. Lionel acquired a very narrow strip of land on the main road into the town, the land lying between that road and a lane sloping steeply up and away from the main road, but running almost parallel to it. There was just room between the building line to the main road and the less onerous building line to the lane to squeeze in a long thin house for the Lionel Jones family on the steeply sloping plot. Indeed, there was also room on the land for a further long thin house on the slightly narrower end of the sliver of land. Dorothy and I were persuaded by Lionel to buy that second morsel of land from him for the grand sum of £125 and to share in the cost of a rather deep sewer connection for the houses tunnelled through solid rock across the main road. We obtained a full planning permission for this second narrow house, but did not go ahead, and still own the land, the planning permission for which has long expired. It can be seen from the drawing that the Corbusier *maison de vaçances* influence was still in operation.

Donald Jones house

Lingard house - not built

The third son Donald did not have a shop. He was the farmer of the family, raising the beasts on rich Anglesey pastures, until ready for the abattoir and on to the shops. I obtained permission for the construction of a new house on several score acres of their pasture land a mile of two out of town and the construction of this house completed my range of commissions for this enterprising Jones family.

Now, much altered, the sketch of the Lionel Jones house is as it was built in the 1950s.

Webster farmhouse

Stone and slate were the traditional building materials in Anglesey until the early years of the 20th century when local brickworks were established and rendered clay common bricks started to replace stone as the material for external walls. Slate had gradually replaced thatch as the traditional material for cottage and farmhouse roofs during the preceding centuries and, because of the proximity of the vast Caernarfonshire slate quarries, slate was cheaper to use for roofs in those days than clay tiles.

Much of the rubble stonework of the old cottages and farmhouses was however rendered over in lime mortar and, even in the 1950s, the first task on site before construction of a new house began, was the digging of the lime pit: the raw lime would be thrown into the pit followed by water, and the lime would then be left to slake in the pit, ready in time to use, mixed with sand, to provide the mortar for the brickwork or stonework and the rendering for the external walls.

For the farmhouses the stonework would be dashed with grey limestone chippings thrown at the wet rendering to provide a surface finish. A variation on that treatment was the mixing of the chippings with a stiff lime and sand mortar, that textured mixture then being thrown at the walls as a last coat. This was termed a rough-cast finish. For the farm buildings, as we have seen, the rubble stonework was usually limewashed every year, this coat upon coat treatment producing a smooth but varying surface following the contours of the large stones lying below. This limewashing technique was also applied sometimes to the roofs of farm buildings where small slates, called peggies, had been used because of the relative cheapness of these slates in earlier days. These smaller slates, parged with horsehair mortar on the underside, tended to be less waterproof than their larger cousins and it was found that a generous application of limewash over the slating year by year would seal the places where wind-blown rain would otherwise penetrate, to drop down on to the animals.

The stone-walling traditions were much in evidence in Anglesey in the mid-20th century, with apprentices still being taken on to continue the trade. Most of the work was however, confined to field or roadside walling or repairs to existing stone buildings. Because of the high labour costs involved in the quarrying, transport and working of the stone, it was rarely possible to build new structures entirely in stone, but I would always endeavour to use some local rubble stonework in houses built outside the towns, either as plinths below ground floor level or as areas of exposed stonework above ground floor level where the design and structure of the dwelling permitted those areas to be seen as an entity, contrasting with the whitewashed rendered areas of brickwork which constituted the main area of external walling. Surprisingly, this use of exposed local uncoursed rubble stonework for new houses was unusual in the island in the 1950s, although this richly textured feature has been much copied by others in later years.

The important points which needed to be observed (one might say 'set in stone') for stonework used in this way were that at least the full 800 mm width of the external wall needed to be exposed in stone on end jambs and that not less than 500 mm thickness of that external wall needed to be in rubble stonework to allow the mason full rein for the placing of larger stones in the wall, even though a lining brick or blockwork skin was used behind to provide a smooth interior for the wall cavity. If these rules were not followed the resulting stonework became little more than external wallpaper.

Other factors (equally 'set in stone') were that the masons had to be urged not to dress the stones too much before building in to the wall, but to select appropriate stones which needed little dressing in order to maintain the 'random' rubble appearance of the walling. Joints between the stones needed to be gouged out heavily to a depth of an inch or so to expose the edges of each stone and were not to be left flush or, still worse, raised above the face of the stonework. These important factors have seldom been observed when stone rubble has been used in recent years for domestic buildings and this rich natural medium has thus often been badly debased.

The Webster family comprised a father and his two sons and they ran a large pig farm outside the village of Gaerwen in the centre of the island. Blunt Yorkshire people, they knew exactly what they wanted for their new house, to be built in front of their present farmhouse. This included the construction of the house entirely in local stone. Their brief for the house, with no compromise possible on the disposition and size of the rooms in the near rectangular plan specified, combined with the absence of any contrast for the stone-walling, resulted in a rather dour dwelling in appearance, but the result is unique in being probably the last house in Anglesey to be built using local stone for the whole of the external walls of the dwelling.

Domestic economy

As a result of the immense post-war reconstruction programme of bomb-damaged cities and the construction of vast numbers of new council houses and schools, a continuous inflation of building costs occurred during the 1950s, accelerating more and more as the decade advanced.

Following the change in government from Labour to Conservative in 1951, the construction of new houses was extended initially to 300,000 in 1953 and then 350,000 in 1954 - an annual total not since exceeded. As the magic figure of £1,000 for a small new two-bedroomed dwelling was reached and passed there was much discussion over the need to keep the figure for these small homes below £1,000 in their building costs.

In the book *New Houses for Moderate Means* mentioned earlier, Dalton Clifford cites the escalation of costs for council house building as:

1949	-	24s 6d sq ft
1951	-	27s 7d sq ft
1955	-	over 30s sq ft

- an increase of 22% at a time when inflation generally was limited to little more than 1% or so a year.

A family of modest means who owned a low-lying pocket-handkerchief sized piece of land in an Anglesey village approached me with these media discussions much in mind. They had no capital and only a limited income but still wondered if it might be possible to put together a dwelling to house their family of five for no more than £1,000, without having to put down a deposit or paying any fees directly. Oh, and the plot was subject to flooding!

The challenge was an interesting one and involved the cutting out of all inessential expenditure on the house by virtually eliminating circulation areas, keeping room sizes to an absolute minimum, adopting the lowest acceptable standards for construction (the roof was covered with slabs of compressed straw) and eschewing all operations which were expensive in labour terms. All this whilst ensuring that the house and approach were raised up above road level to combat the flooding, that the result was compatible with building bye-law requirements, and that it would receive a detailed planning permission on environmental grounds.

The problems did not, however, end there. It was necessary to ensure that the completed dwelling would qualify for a 100% mortgage for the building costs and fees, using the value of the tiny piece of land as the 'deposit' in the package. That mortgage was obtained for the family through the aegis of a helpful local mortgage broker and the house was built, including an admittedly skimpy fee for architectural services, within the £1,000 mortgage limit. The family were thus housed adequately in this new cottage, equipped with all modern facilities at a price they could afford within their modest means and at no expense to the state.

The £1,000 expended to create this small house is the equivalent of over £30,000 in 21st century terms.

Beesley ferry house

The ferries between Anglesey and the mainland continued to operate across the Menai Straits long after the construction of the Telford and Stephenson bridges which linked the island with the mainland in the middle years of the 19th century. Indeed, when Dorothy and I went to live in Anglesey there were four such ferries still plying between Bangor and Beaumaris, Bangor and Glyn Garth, Portdinorwic and Min-y-Don and between Caernarfon and Brynsiencyn at the western end of the Straits. They were perpetuated by ancient Acts of Parliament which placed responsibility upon the Anglesey County Council for maintaining the daily ferry links at a cost of no more than one or two pence a crossing. Other than for holiday trips, one of the most used of the ferries after the construction of the bridges was the Brynsiencyn to Caernarfon ferry which made Caernarfon the most accessible town to the agricultural population of the south-eastern corner of the island, far more direct than the alternative 20-mile road journey, firstly to Menai Bridge and then on down the Caernarfonshire side of the Straits to Caernarfon. Livestock were transported to market across the ferry and there was a good traffic in household goods and farm produce by the same route.

The ferry house at the landing point of the Caernarfon ferry in Anglesey comprised a house for the ferry master with a large storeroom attached for holding goods awaiting transport over the Straits to Caernarfon on the ferry boat. There was an inn adjacent to the ferry house where passengers could obtain refreshments whilst awaiting the next ferry or to recover from the often quite treacherous mile-long sea journey by open boat.

The ferries were clearly uneconomic in the mid-20th century and the County Council eventually succeeded with a Parliamentary Bill permitting their closure, other than for maintaining the Bangor crossings during the summer months for the tourist trade. The Portdinorwic and Caernarfon ferry houses on the Anglesey side of the Menai Straits were then put on the market.

Friends from Cheshire came to visit us in Anglesey from time to time, generally during the August holiday season, but one couple for whom Dorothy and I had acted as bridesmaid and groomsman at their wedding were the Beesleys who lived in Prestbury. Don Beesley was in the roofing business and had connections with North Wales slate quarries, requiring him to come to North Wales several times each year to visit the quarries.

Don and Joanne Beesley heard about the unusual ferry house at Brynsiencyn and acquired the buildings and the associated stone jetty forming the little high water harbour. Their next step was to ask me to draw up plans for the renovation of the buildings with modern amenities and the conversion of the large storeroom to become part of the living accommodation. The storeroom, with large windows built-in to capture the magnificent views across the Straits to Caernarfon Castle and the mountains beyond, became the living area for the new house, with the heavy pine planks which formed the warehouse floor being caulked with hemp and pitch before sanding, to form (with a scattering of rugs) a most appropriate and substantial floor for this large maritime room.

Part of the attraction of this remote corner of the island was the fact that the adjoining inn, once the haunt of ferry passengers, had passed into the hands of a Liverpool businessman and his wife who, at a time when good restaurant food was hard to find in Britain, created a cuisine which came to hold almost national renown. Indeed, in the earliest years of the *Good Food Guide*, first published by Raymond Postgate in 1951, directions were given on how to reach The Mermaid Inn, as it had been renamed, from London. 'Take the Edgware Road and follow the A5 for 260 miles from Marble Arch then turn left after crossing Telford's bridge over the Menai Straits'.

The landlord pursued his business in Liverpool during the week, returning to Anglesey each weekend, whilst his wife looked after the inn alone on weekdays, serving dinner to a full house of 20 or 30 covers each evening despite the isolated position. This most successful restaurant continued in operation for several years until the early sixties when there was a breach in the marriage, with local talk of socks belonging to chef having been found in the marital bed one weekend.

The Beesley family continued to use their ferry house holiday home for many years until the children grew up and the house was passed on for others to enjoy this magnificent site.

PERCENTAGE FEES NURTURE GOOD DESIGN

Cemlyn Jones house

The RIBA Code of Professional Conduct in the 1950s was very strict. Members were not allowed to advertise in any way or to 'tout' for business. They were obliged to conform to the precise Scale of Charges for their fees to ensure that they did not undercut any of their fellow RIBA members. In other words, they were obliged to sit in their offices and to wait for clients to come forward on the basis of recommendations from friends, relatives or past clients alone. Once established, this was a fair basis for an architectural private practice in that it ensured that commissions were obtained purely on the basis of reputation and not on the lowest fee bid. High standards of design and detail were thus achieved and maintained as a result of these regulations but it was very hard for a young architect to found a practice against the background of these restrictions.

Most of my early single house commissions were gained as the result of personal contacts and it was most encouraging, after the construction of these first few houses to see new commissions coming forward from hitherto unknown individuals. One such early commission came from the daughter of a well-known land-owning family from the north of the island.

Miss Cemlyn Jones had aquired a plot of land and the wherewithal to build herself a new house in Menai Bridge. The commission was for a large house on a site high above the village, sloping away towards the south-east and enjoying the magnificent views of the Straits and Snowdownia referred to in an earlier vignette. The residents of Anglesey often boasted that the best views of the Caernarfonshire mountains were to be obtained from vantage points on their island of Ynys Mon.

The position chosen for the house on this site involved some excavation in solid rock, as can be judged from the photograph and, indeed, the house was built entirely on a rock foundation, providing a firm base for the structure. Such an excellent foundation was not always found, but it is a fallacy of people in general (other than for architects and masterbuilders who have experience of many completed buildings) that, once built, a new building is a rigid, immutable whole and that the appearance of one or two minute cracks in a wall surface is equivalent to Armageddon!

It was necessary to explain over and again to different building owners that a traditional building is almost akin to a living being; that the enormous quantities of water which go into the construction of concrete floors, the brickwork or stonework and the plastering and rendering of the walling will not dry out entirely for a year or two after the completion of the building and that this may well result in shrinkage cracks appearing in wall surfaces; that timbers used in construction, although kiln dried to quite low levels of moisture content, can shrink still further given the aggressive use of a central heating system; that daily and seasonal variations in external temperature will expand and contract the materials used in construction; that winter rains and storms will introduce more moisture into the building fabric which cannot dry out properly until the summer, producing yet further expansion and contraction of the structure; and that minor settlement of the structural walls on the concrete foundations, or of the foundations themselves on the sub-soil, can produce slight distortions in the building fabric over quite a long period after construction.

All of these matters can produce minor fissures in the structure, almost all of which have little or no consequence in relation to the stability of the building and which can be filled and painted out at a subsequent decoration, probably never to appear again.

The growing compensation culture of our society however, often sees these minor movements in a living building as the opportunity for a substantial claim, on the basis that the slightest crack in a wall surface is signal that the structure is about to collapse and that it must involve the complete replacement, or extensive strengthening, of the foundations in order to prevent Armageddon. None of this applied to the Cemlyn Jones house which, with a foundation in sold rock, did indeed remain immutable.

CATTLE MARKET ECONOMICS

Owen Hughes house

A few days after moving in to our 'new' house at Rhydysbardyn in the autumn of 1950, there was a knock at the back door in the early evening. In the darkness stood a short thick-set man who introduced himself as a Mr Hughes. He said that he would like to talk to us about our occupation of Rhydysbardyn. Rather reluctantly we asked him to come into the house but he refused despite the chill of the autumn evening. He nevertheless wished to continue his conversation from the doorstep.

It transpired that he was a cattle dealer and that he had been most anxious to acquire Rhydysbardyn and particularly the eleven acres of well-watered grazing land which surrounded the house. As he brought in his cattle to market or the abattoir in Llangefni the land was well placed, little more than a mile or so away from the market, to hold the cattle if prices were not quite right for selling or killing. We had obviously trodden on Mr Hughes' toes as he believed that he would otherwise have obtained the property for the odd hundred or two pounds less than we had paid.

He was anxious to know whether we would be prepared to sell Rhydysbardyn on to him and, if so, how much did we want to make the move?

Having spent several months converting and modernizing the interior of the house (including a nursery for our imminent first-born!) the last thing we were thinking about was making a move for several years and we said that, as we had spent a good deal of money on the house, we would need to receive far more than it was worth to make a move. A rather disgruntled Mr Hughes then moved away into the gloom without having set foot in the house.

A year or two later we were interested to learn from the local paper that a large area of grazing land on the road leading from Llangefni to the junction with the A5 had been sold to a Mr Hughes, without making the connection - there are a lot of Mr Hugheses in Anglesey.

A month or two later however, I met our Mr Hughes for a second time - on this occasion in my office, when he revealed himself as being the owner of the 50 acres which had been the subject of the sale. He would like to have a house for himself and his family, building on the land what would nominally be a 'farmhouse', but with no associated farm buildings.

Owen Hughes turned out to be an excellent client, with a generous budget and a desire to ensure that what was to become the first house to be seen by a visitor coming by the main road to the county town was a credit to himself and the community. One firm instruction however, in the tradition of all Anglesey farmers, was that the external walls of the house were to be stone dashed, but that I could use rubble stonework for the plinth, the garage and the screen walls.

Many years later the house was extended by others and this has badly disturbed the balance of the original composition, but the photograph illustrates the house as it appeared on the completion of the original contract. The rather ornate iron gates were by a blacksmith friend of the farmer and were not part of the contract.

FORCE 9 GALES AND A GHOSTLY WELL

Fletcher butterfly house

In the inter-war years there had been a growth in the 'railway' holiday villages of Rhosneigr, Trearddur Bay and Red Wharf Bay where the railways came close to the beaches, with families building holiday houses for their own use during August each year. One of the earliest books of Nicholas Monsarrat (of *The Cruel Sea* fame) was a slim volume written in honour of his brother, who was killed during the war, called *My Brother Denys* (Chariot Books, 1948). The book painted a fascinating word picture of this pre-war superimposition of English families on Welsh-speaking Anglesey during the summer months.

The building of new holiday houses in Anglesey was slow to revive after the war, mostly because of the licensing restrictions which were in force until the end of 1954. It was thus still possible in the 1950s to acquire quite large plots of land close to the seashore for the construction of single dwellings and this house, built for Mr and Mrs Fletcher is an early example of a postwar holiday house built on the cliffs close to Trearddur Bay.

Only a small 'cottage' was to be built on this large, bleak, heather-covered area of cliff and the 'butterfly' roof was intended to give an emphasis to the structure which was otherwise in danger of being overwhelmed visually by the severe coastal environment. During these early years in private architectural practice I was conscious of my inexperience in practical building matters and my policy was to say as little as possible at meetings with builders and sub-contractors until I had had a chance to consult the text books on particular matters of detail which were under consideration. I thus relied much, in these early years, on the building foremen or the owner of the contracting firm for practical advice on detail, particularly on sites exposed to the prevailing, rain-saturated, south-westerly gales fresh off the Irish Sea.

I was particularly indebted to Glyn Jones, proprietor of Henry Jones and Sons, the contractors for this house who, when taking on the implications of the butterfly roof on this exposed site advised that, at each corner of the building, we should build in steel rods, coach-screwed to the timber roof structure and then taken down several feet before turning and embedding them into the brickwork of the external walls. Otherwise, I was informed by Glyn Jones, the whole of the roof would be in the Irish Sea at the first force 9 westerly gale!

I can remember the restless night spent listening to the howling fury of that first force 9 and my 6am first-light visit to Trearddur Bay to satisfy myself that the roof was not floating in the sea on its way to Ireland. All was safe and sound however and I had learnt a useful detail to adopt for all new roofs to be built in exposed coastal positions.

The construction of this house was badly delayed because, at the first sign of building activity on the site, the nearest neighbours obtained an injunction to prevent further building operations on the grounds that their deeds showed a right-of-way for them across our site to the position of a well for which they held the right-of-way to draw their drinking water. This was despite the fact that there was now a mains water supply to the house and that no sign of a well could be found where indicated on the deeds. The neighbours were, of course, not at all bothered about the water supply but were determined to avoid even the minor interruption to their view which would occur with the construction of the new cottage.

The lawyers enjoyed a beanfeast and their expensive proceedings were only brought to a halt by a wise County Court judge who told the parties to go away and lock themselves into a room together until they had decided to not bother him again over the dispute, other than to tell him that the action had been withdrawn. The neighbours withdrew their claim and building work resumed after a six-month delay. I understand that the adjoining owners subsequently became good friends and never referred to the matter again.

GLYN GARTH PEOPLE

McKenzie house from the lower drive

Ronald McKenzie was a chartered surveyor and was the proprietor of John Pritchard & Co, a leading estate agent in north-west Wales. With his wife and two daughters he lived in a remarkable old stone-built house clinging to the wooded slopes of the shore line in Glyn Garth on a relatively narrow, steeply sloping strip of land lying between the coast road and the high-water mark. Their house was the last in Glyn Garth before the woodlands of the Bulkeley estate took over the coastline for the next mile or two into Beaumaris. The house, in company with the handful of other houses which clung to the cliffline in Glyn Garth in a similar manner, enjoyed private, sheltered, deep-water moorings immediately below the windows of the house.

Despite the magnificent position of the fine house, the McKenzies felt the need for rather more useable grounds around the house and for more modern accommodation. When some six acres of nearby parkland, on the upper side of the coastal road came onto the market, this was exactly the site they had been waiting for and it was acquired complete with an Eton Fives court, a Twr and a stone icehouse buried in the woodland, all relics from a grand previous house on the site which had been demolished many years before.

There was difficulty in determining a precise site for the house with six acres to choose from, but a position was eventually settled close to the top of the site to take advantage of the fine views along the Straits. A 100-yard long hairpin-shaped drive was constructed up from the main coastal road, giving a good prospect of the house and grounds on the way up the drive.

The accommodation provided in this single-storey house was a generous entrance hall with cloakroom, drawing room, large kitchen with dining bay, sun room, four bedrooms and two bathrooms. A spacious garage with room for four cars was provided by the roofing-in of the nearby Fives court. All, I recollect, for just over £7,000 in 1955. By this time building licences had faded into memory, development charges had disappeared and all building materials, including timber and steel, were available, with careful forward planning, for private house building.

From the upper drive

The entrance at night

View from the south-west to the Straits and mountains

Teddy Rye garage

This book deals essentially with new dwellings built from the ground up or involving comprehensive remodelling from older structures but it would be inappropriate not to mention the major part which the houses of Glyn Garth played in the establishment of my architectural practice in the 1950s and early 1960s.

Apart from a small area of land around the ferry house serving the then still extant Glyn Garth/Bangor ferry across the Straits, the shoreline at Glyn Garth rose steeply from the water's edge, across unstable, clay-rooted woodland, to the coastal road some 30 to 40 feet above and just 50 or 60 feet away from high-water mark. Despite these difficult conditions, several houses had been built in the early half of the century clinging to the cliff face below the road - a sort of prototype for the development of Malibu beach in California by Hollywood film people! Some of my earliest commissions were for the construction of garages for these dwellings, which had not been provided previously but which were now essential for mid-20th century living.

One of these garages is illustrated here and the difficulties of the site can be well appreciated from the photograph. Teddy Rye, the client for this new garage was a Liverpool cotton merchant who had spent several years immediately pre-war building up his house from the beach layer by layer and floor by floor from building materials which he sailed in to the foot of the site on barges from across the Straits.

Another early client for a garage in Glyn Garth was the Chairman of the Anglesey County Council who had a house, without garage, almost adjoining the Rye house. Fortunately, the under-building required was rather less and the result was a more conventional garage.

During the course of that contract, my client acquired a new motor car, which bore the registration number BEY1 (EY being the Anglesey registration letters). The very first car to be registered in Anglesey was owned by the Bulkeley family and Sir Richard's motor still carried the unique EY1 registration number. Not to be too outdone, Lord Anglesey had acquired the AEY1 number immediately the county progressed from two to three letter registrations in the late 1940s.

Being acquainted with the County Council Licensing Officer, I discussed this interesting progression of registration numbers with him and wondered whether CEY 1 might soon be available. He told me that that registration number had been reserved by the Governor of what was then Ceylon.

Thinking rather a long way forward, I came to KEY 1 and it occured to me that this might be a good number for an architect and said so to my friend; I had already handed the key of the door of their new house to many families in the early 1950s.

Some years later a telephone call was received from the County Council to say that they had reached KEY 1 and would I like to have the number. As it happened, a new car was due to be delivered a week or two later and it thus bore the KEY 1 number, one which I transferred from car to car over many years before the registration numbers' game became something of a rather unhealthy cult, at which time I passed on the 'Key' of my last car to carry that number as part of the part-exchange deal with my garage, for, I suspect, rather more than the box of a hundred cigarettes which I had passed to my licensing officer friend.

Another early client with a Glyn Garth building problem was Commander Alan Jones who owned a mid-19th century house built flush with the edge of the coastal road but on the landward side of that road. The steepness of the site can be judged by the fact that the roof of the house, at fourth-storey level, was level with the bottom of the terraced garden lying immediately behind the house. The problem which was posed by Commander Jones was the building of a new flat roof above the existing pitched roofs to form a garden roof terrace bridged to the rear garden area on the same level and commanding unsurpassed views of the Straits and the mountains. This involved taking off the top of some of the pitched roofs and despite choosing June as the ideal month for the operations, it proved to be a stormy month. I can recollect, in response to a telephone call of desperation from the client, turning out in the middle of one stormy night to clamber over the un-scaffolded roofs 50 feet above road level to assist the hastily summoned builder in reinstating tarpaulins (which had been torn off by the gale) in order to stop the flooding of the house below. These are not the kind of duties for the architect which tend to figure in the RIBA Code of Professional Conduct.

Dr Lloyd house

In the mid-1950s, with two very active young men, aged four and two, making the limited accommodation at Rhydysbardyn seem even more restricted and with the work of the architectural practice spreading further out into North Wales, Dorothy and I decided to move our house and my personal work-base down the coast to Colwyn Bay. Before contemplating that move however, it was necessary to find a cottage in Anglesey in which to live during the parts of the year when we expected to stay in Anglesey. A small cottage on the outskirts of Rhosneigr called Glan Morfa (the cottage on the marsh) came on the market and was to be sold at auction. The cottage was without modern amenities and was a simple Anglesey crogloft cottage with two rooms on the ground floor and a loft bedroom over one of the rooms in the roof space. The living room side had no ceiling and was open to the rafters. As the cottage was close by the Anglesey Golf Club clubhouse however, it was expected that it would attract a good deal of attention at auction.

This proved to be the case, with the lounge bar at the Bay Hotel packed to the doors awaiting the auctioneer. We had a figure of £500 in mind for our limit and our hearts sank to see the size of the assembled crowd. Bidding started at £350 and went briskly up to £500 without our having had a chance to bid. We did however, with some trepidation, enter the fray at £550 and eventually secured Glan Morfa at £625, which local opinion was quick to inform us was greatly in excess of the correct value. I recall that our opponent on the last few steps of the bidding was the Senior Executive of the University of Bangor who was also looking for a pied-à-terre in Rhosneigr. Bang goes any chance of a commission for the practice from the University was my first thought after the hammer fell.

The next step was the location of a suitable house combined with office in Colwyn Bay but, before that had been achieved, an offer was received for Rhydysbardyn which was impossible to resist and we contented ourselves with the fact that, by then, we had almost completed work at Glan Morfa and we could spend a month or two there whilst the Colwyn Bay house was located. The move out of Rhydysbardyn was made on 20 June 1954 on which day the sun came out after a rainy spring and it shone, without a break, from then on until the end of the first week in September.

Our young sons, not yet of school age, spent most of the next ten weeks on the beaches and in the sea, throughout that glorious summer, but we were then reminded of the approach of winter in September when the birds massed along the roof tops and telephone wires of the village ready for their annual migration south - and still no suitable Colwyn Bay house in sight.

Glan Morfa proved to be most unsuitable for a family winter residence. Small and cramped, with solid stone walls and quarry tile floors, all in the teeth of the cold, wet south-westerlies off the Irish Sea. The Colwyn Bay house was acquired late in 1954 but alterations and renovations were needed and the builders did not start work until the early spring.

We all needed the attention of a doctor during that winter, with colds, coughs, flu and other ailments. Dr Denys Lloyd was the newly appointed junior doctor of a partnership based in Gwalchmai in the centre of the island. He assumed responsibility for the Rhosneigr part of the practice and needed a house for his young family and associated surgery/waiting-room accommodation in the village. I had been designing a small estate of houses for Henry Jones & Sons, the contractors based in the village, and had left two plots of land on the frontage of the site for special one-off dwellings. This house and surgery was designed for the Lloyds on one of the plots and they were moved in to their new house within just a few months of first arriving in the village. It was very comforting to be in such constant close touch with our local doctor during this difficult winter.

The Colwyn Bay house was ready for occupation in early September 1955 and that winter proved to be a good deal more comfortable and ailment-free for our family than the previous winter.

GOD WILL PROVIDE

Menai Bridge Catholic church

A church cannot strictly be regarded as being in the special houses for special people category but it is nevertheless a special house for a Special Being. As that superior form of house it can therefore qualify for inclusion in this book!

In the mid-1950s I was approached by the owner of one of the fine houses lying close to Menai Bridge which each occupy a substantial frontage of the Anglesey shore of the Menai Straits. A Roman Catholic, he was concerned that there was no place of worship for the Catholic community in Menai Bridge. He had located, and purchased, a site close to the centre of the village, had made a handsome donation to the building fund and had twisted the arm of the chairman of a major regional contracting firm (Pochins) who specialised in high-class joinery work, to build the church quickly and at low cost.

I was asked to design and supervise the construction of this modest little church.

The site was an interesting one, occupying a piece of land in the centre of the village which had remained undeveloped because of the way in which it sloped steeply up away from the road frontage. The rocky site was also blessed with some fine mature pines which needed to be protected and nurtured if at all possible.

Towards the end of my architectural student days in Manchester, and being interested in structural design, I had also followed evening courses at the University of Manchester Institute of Science and Technology which led to the final examination of the Institute of Structural Engineers. Although completing the course in 1949, I deferred the taking of the examinations at the same time as my final architectural exams but then, after getting married that summer, the opportunity of continuing with the structural engineering studies did not again arise. Nevertheless, my interest in the relationship of structural engineering to architecture remained a lifetime one and, in this little church, I was able to introduce the principle of timber, plywood-clad, rigid portal-frame construction to support the roof of the nave, which also provided an interesting sculptural quality for the church interior.

This commission for a new Roman Catholic church was followed by a succession of further commissions for church work throughout North Wales from the Bishop of Menevia, including a similar new church in Rhosneigr, also illustrated here.

Rhosneigr Catholic church

Knowing that the Menai Bridge church had been funded largely by private donations, I was interested to learn from where the money was to come for the new Rhosneigr church. That interest had been stimulated by a recent visit to my office by a lady who announced that she proposed to build a village for a religious community '...on the slopes of Snowdon' and wished to know whether I would act for her in that matter. There was no specific site for the village in view and I ventured the opinion that there might be some difficulty with the planning authority over the introduction of a new village on the slopes of Snowdon. Enquiring more closely into the concept, I asked from where the money was to come to fund the construction of the village and was told that 'God will provide'. Needless to say, this prospective commission was not one which was pursued further by my office!

When asking much the same question of the parish priest for Rhosneigr however, I received the more practical answer that the football pool which was run by the church on the island would soon provide the necessary funds. This proved to be quite so, and here perhaps was the kind of model which John Major had in mind when establishing the National Lottery many years later.

*Glenroyd - our home from
1955 - 1962*

The Misses Brown were two sisters who lived in Rhosneigr and who had obtained for themselves a small plot of land on a residential road on the edge of the village. One sister worked as a secretary and commuted to Bangor each day on the train and the other sister looked after their home. They proved to be difficult clients to work with in the approval of design drawings, having rigid views on the character of the house they required. The house was thus a little uninspired, albeit plain and honest in appearance. No as-built photograph was taken and the recent construction of an unfortunate large glazed porch straddled across the main frontage precludes the use of a present day image. The photograph is thus of a different 'special' house.

During construction, matters became worse, with constant telephone calls being received concerning minor details of finishings, almost on a daily basis. Towards the end of the contract there had been an accumulation of such uncleared matters and there was a need for a meeting at which all the many outstanding points could be inspected, discussed and settled. This was arranged for mid-morning at the house on a day when I was going to be in Rhosneigr for another later engagement.

As soon as the meeting opened it became clear that the session was going to be a long one. The sisters were seeking far higher standards in the work of the contractor than was justified and the architect was subjected to severe criticism for not having instructed the removal of virtually the entire interior of the house and the replacement of all joinery, plumbing, plastering and tiling work! I exaggerate, but there was nothing for it but detailed inspection, discussion and decision concerning each of the individual 40 plus items on the Brown list.

Hour after hour passed in this way but, lunchless (!) at 2.30 pm I had to suspend the discussions (or rather arguments) and leave to go straight to another meeting in Rhosneigr for which I was already running half-an-hour late. I promised to return and did so at 4pm for a strained further two hours or so.

Arriving back at our Rhosneigr cottage, I had only a few minutes to wash, shave, change into a dinner jacket and set off again for the officers' mess of the nearby army missile-testing station for a cocktail party ahead of the Rhosneigr Golf Club annual dinner and dance which was to be held that evening. After a difficult day, the first gin and tonic did indeed live up to the latter part of the title of the mixture, although it tasted rather strong. A second was quickly proffered and accepted but, knowing that my driving limit was three normal gin and tonics, I eased up, yet pressed by the generous hospitality of the army, a third was accepted before everybody prepared to leave for the dinner venue several miles away.

What I had not appreciated was that army tots of spirits were three or four times the normal size. Hitting the night air and sitting behind the wheel of the car, for the first and last time in my life, I realised that I was in no fit state to drive and I handed over the wheel to Dorothy. My stomach, empty since breakfast time had ensured that the three generous pourings of alcohol had gone straight into my bloodstream. I did not reach the dinner or the dance that evening, defeated by a combination of five hours of the Brown snagging lists, an absence of food all day and the hidden generosity of the army pourings. The day has thus remained strongly in my memory since that time as a supreme example of the difficulties which can arise in resolving the minor contractual disputes occurring during a simple one-off house contract.

The problems of architect/client relationship on residential projects are defined admirably by José Manser in her biography of Hugh Casson, *Hugh Casson - a Biography* (Viking Books, 2000). Mrs Manser is the wife of Michael Manser, an architect and past-president of the RIBA and she has thus a penetrating view of such relationships through the eyes of her husband. She says:

> "The client-architect relationship is a notoriously difficult one, never more so than when it centres on residential projects. Architects can become arrogant and overly convinced of their design invincibility when faced with what they come to regard as intractable clients, forgetting that it is the client's money they are involving in pursuance of their grand schemes. And some clients get so emotionally involved with what is being done to their property that they consider it the architect's single concern: even late on a Sunday evening when he's...neither equipped nor eager to enter into long detailed discussions on the telephone. Tales of architect inadequacies or client transgressions on the residential front are legion, and the number of such connections which end in recrimination, anger or even a law suit is high."

In the absence of a Brown house illustration, a photograph of our house and office in Colwyn Bay at this time is shown, the special people here being my wife Dorothy, our two small sons and, in due course, our baby daughter.

23

A PINT AND A CHOP

Phoenix

My first visit to Llangefni, the County Town of Anglesey, was made in the 1930s. My father had business connections in North Wales and was wont to visit Llangefni once or twice a year in pursuance of those interests. I accompanied him occasionally, staying a night in Llandudno, Caernarfon and Aberystwyth en route. Although a county town, Llangefni in those pre-war years was barely a village, with a population of about 1,800 souls, in comparison with the normal definition for a 'town' in more populous parts of Great Britain. The stone-built 17th century Bull Hotel formed the centre-piece to the town, occupying one side of the market square.

George Borrows in his book *Wild Wales*, recording his tour of Wales which was conducted largely on foot in 1854, recollects that, after visiting the ancestral home of the Tudors at Penmynydd a mile or two outside the town, he walked to Llangefni and described it as a '...small, neat town' and what is now called the Bull Hotel as a '... magnificent structure'. He went into the hotel and ordered '... a pint and chop' for his lunch and was surprised to be served a pint of sherry rather than his intended pint of ale. When he explained the error he was told that they did not expect a gentleman to mean ale when ordering a pint. He drank the sherry with his chop however and then walked to Holyhead in the afternoon - no doubt zig-zagging a little along the lanes! An old hardwood notice was still displayed in the stone-flagged entrance hall of the hotel in 1950 setting out the rules of the house, one of which instructed guests that they should not wear spurs in bed.

Llew Hughes house

The Bull Hotel Llangefni

Next to the Bull Hotel was the town hall, with the under-part having the weekly market on the ground floor and the hall on the first floor. An archway close to the Market Square led down into the cattle market, held every Wednesday. On the corner of Market Square and Church Street was the premises of Hugh Hughes and Sons, Ironmongers and Builders Merchants. The current holder of the business was Llew Hughes, with whom my father had his business.

A few days after arriving in Anglesey, Dorothy and I called on Llew Hughes to introduce ourselves and we were warmly welcomed. A few months later I thought that it would be prudent to seek his advice, as an authority on the building trade on the island, on the propects for an architect in private practice in the town. He thought the prospects to be good, with the nearest chartered architect being in Bangor, outside the island.

I was then delighted when, a few years later, Llew Hughes asked me to design a new house for his family on a plot which lay in the same lane as the Lionel Jones' house, higher up the lane and on the opposite side of the road.

Sadly, Llew Hughes never moved into the house. He died suddenly just after work started on the house and his family decided not to continue with the contract in these circumstances. All that is left of the original design are the drawings, and a sketch of the front elevation is illustrated here. The photograph shows the attractive house which was built on the foundations by others, using the walls which had been constructed up to ground floor level as the base - but to a different design and by a different architect.

24

GALES, TIDES, SEA-SPRAY AND WIND-BLOWN SAND

Britten house

Charles Britten was a motor-showroom proprietor who had the Liverpool agency for one of our principal motor manufacturers in the 1950s. Being close to retirement he sold the premises and the agency for, I recollect, a sum in excess of a quarter of a million pounds - the equivalent of nearly £10 million in today's funny money. Being a keen dinghy sailor he chose Rhosneigr as his retirement home and managed to acquire one of the few remaining beach frontage plots.

He was aware that when the wind was from the south-west (the direction the site faced across the beach) and the tides were high, a house in that position would receive much battering from wind, rain, sea spray and wind-blown sand. My instructions were therefore to ensure that all the elements of the building were exceptionally hardy, sturdy, windproof and rainproof.

The first consideration was the boundary walls, particularly on the sea side of the property. That boundary was marked only by a straggling post and wire fence just above high-water mark and set in the beginnings of the small sandhills which comprised the site. My instructions were to ensure that the foundations of the boundary walls were taken down well below high-water mark level and, because of the moving tidal sub-soil water level, the concrete strip foundations were heavily reinforced. The boundary wall itself was constructed in 800 mm thick local stone rubble walling set in waterproof cement mortar and extending to some 1.2 metres above ground level. At high spring tides, assisted by a force 9, south-westerly gale, the wall would be subject to direct attack from the waves rolling up the beach. The name of the house - Random - was chosen by the clients as a result of the constant references to the 'random rubble walling' used in the construction of these important defensive walls. The external walls of the dwelling were to be sand-coloured hard-burnt, clay-facing bricks, or spar-dashed rendering, using a full brick width for the external skin of the cavity wall on the sea side of the dwelling.

The roof was to be of seconds Dinorwic slates, which were heavier than firsts, and the windows were stipulated as vertical sash windows in hardwood, requiring no painting. The type of hardwood to be used was discussed with the client. The available hardwoods in those early postwar years were Meranti, Sapele and Iroko from West Africa at about twice the price of softwood. They were useful woods but did not have the character and staying power of the universally used, pre-war hardwoods such as English Oak or Honduras Mahogany. Burma Teak was the supreme timber for external joinery work and I had heard that a Liverpool firm had recommenced the limited import of this renowned hardwood quite recently. Enquiries revealed that it would be possible to import sufficient teak for our needs, but at a price between two and three times that of West African hardwood. This news was conveyed to the client in an apologetic manner, but the immediate response was 'get it'! The windows at Random are therefore all in best Burma Teak, looking today more or less exactly as they were nearly 50 years ago, with only an occasional wiping down and light oiling necessary to keep them in pristine condition.

All this attention to robust and uncompromising materials and detailing, whilst fulfilling the requirement of the brief for hardiness and sturdyness, resulted in a rather plain and unromantic house, but Random was certainly one of the 'firmest' houses to emerge from my office drawing boards.

The house from the beach

After taking up the whole of the sea frontage of the land for the Britten house, there was sufficient room left between the rear garden area of the house and Rhosneigr High Street for two more houses and the plot immediately behind the house was sold to Mr and Mrs Charters, for whom I designed a more modest holiday home, served from the grassy lane which led down from the High Street to the Britten house and the shore beyond; a house which is now much altered and extended.

25

YELLOW ROLLS ROYCE

Partington house

Tom Partington spent the early years of his life living at Bramall Hall in Cheshire - one of the finest examples of historic half-timbered houses in the country, standing in some 50 acres of ornamental grounds. Simon Jenkins in his book *England's Thousand Best Houses* cites Bramall Hall as being his favourite amongst Cheshire's (many) black and white houses - a most special house! The house and grounds were passed over to the local authority for public use in the 1920s and the family moved to the Dower House in the grounds of the Hall. Their summer residence, Orme Lodge, was at the western end of the promenade in Llandudno and was the house to where Alice Liddell's family (of *Alice in Wonderland*) came from Oxford to spend each August in their early years in Llandudno. Llandudno always knew when the Partington family was in residence as Tom's mother would be seen to sally forth in her open-backed, chauffeur-driven, yellow Rolls Royce in and about the resort.

Alice Liddell house

Tom married and he and his new wife decided to move from the Dower House and to build themselves a more manageable residence at Gannock Park in Deganwy. Gannock Park, climbing up the slope of the Vadre 'mountain' behind Deganwy, with each house enjoying extensive views out across the estuary of the Conwy river to the mountains and on to Anglesey in the west, is one of the most environmentally successful private housing estates in the country, certainly in North Wales. The estate owners in the inter-war years laid out the land in wide, tree-lined roadways and stipulated a minimum size of about a quarter of an acre for the plots, not to be sub-divided. Substantial boundary walls were to be built in local stone and houses were to be detached and were to hold a minimum floor area. Most of the 40 or 50 or so plots of land were developed with fine houses by 1940 and only pockets of land remained for the completion of the estate after the war years. The plot which was secured by the Partingtons lay towards the foot of the estate, not commanding the extensive views of the upper houses, but nevertheless enjoying attractive glimpses of the estuary and the mountains beyond through the trees.

Dorothy and I had known the Partington family when they lived in Bramhall, being members of the same tennis club and one of our great friends had married Tom's brother George. It cannot therefore be said that this commission for a new house came to me purely on the basis of architectural reputation but such nepotic commissions are the lifeblood of an emerging architectural practice!

Tom Partington knew exactly what he wanted for the content and appearance of the new house, requirements which did not exactly fit in with my own feelings for post-war domestic architecture. With friends however, if friends an architect wishes them to remain, compromise must be in the air and this was a house which was much compromised in the details of the design. Nevertheless, the result was a comfortable and well-built dwelling and the friendship was not disturbed. Indeed, as coincidences happen, our younger son, a few years later, found himself at the same school in Shropshire, the same house and the same year as George Partington's son Christopher, which has kept us in touch with the Partington family ever since!

The Burns cottage and extension

John Burns was a dentist from Liverpool who had bought, with his wife Monica, a tiny cottage right in the centre of Rhosneigr village, set at an angle to a road leading directly down to the beach and amongst a group of newer houses. An extension was needed to the cottage to house their young family for holidays and this I designed to lie across the garden, ranged at a slight angle to the existing cottage.

The recommendation to use me as their architect for this extension had come from a fellow architect, George Grenfell-Baines, the senior partner in what was to become the largest architectural practice in the UK, Building Design Partnership (now the seventh largest architectural firm in the world). I had known George Baines since student days when he had come to lecture my year on professional practice matters. In 1954 I had designed and built a new premises for a wine merchant in Llangefni to replace a small warehouse in the High Street and had planned offices at the first floor level, which I then took on a 21-year lease in replacement for my first tiny office on the other side of the High Street.

About the same time Grenfell-Baines had bought a house for use by the partners of his practice at Wern-y-Wylan overlooking Red Wharf Bay. This was one of a group of houses and an hotel and shop built by Sir Harry Verney on part of his land immediately before the war. Wern-y-Wylan was an architecturally attractive scheme enjoying fine views over bracken-covered slopes to the vast expanse of the sands of Red Wharf Bay below. Sir Harry attracted much publicity for his holiday village when he erected roadside signs drawing attention to the location of his hotel and advertising 'Teas <u>without</u> Hovis', for which he was sued by the Hovis company.

On a visit to Llangefni, George was attracted by the new wine shop and offices, saw the brass plate and called in. Thereafter we usually met for lunch once a year or so when he was on the island and we remained in touch for many years. He was an ardent Socialist and I recall passing a journey from London to Crewe with him on the train when his light reading matter was revealed to be Karl Marx's *Das Kapital*. Nevertheless, or perhaps because of these views he went on to become a Vice-President of the RIBA and Sir George Grenfell-Baines.

Lingard office, Langefni

Going back to the Burns' cottage, this was completed in time for the summer school holidays in 1954 and was much enjoyed by the family that year. The Burns were visited by Monica's father and mother during the course of the summer and they were attracted immediately to Rhosneigr. Father was Noel Le Mare who always confided to people that, when young, he had three ambitions in life - to marry a beautiful wife, to become a millionaire and to win the Grand National - the inference being that he had already achieved the first two and was well on the way to achieving the third. In fact, he went on to win the Grand National three times in succession with his horse Red Rum in the 1970s.

Le Mare house

Noel Le Mare was Chairman of Norwest Construction, a contracting firm he had built up from an early succession of contracts which he told me comprised the digging by hand, with a gang of Irish labourers, of hundreds of miles of trenches undergrounding telephone lines from their poles alongside main roads. Norwest Construction went on to become one of the major building contracting firms in the country (later Norwest Holst). Hence the relationship with Grenfell-Baines.

The Le Mares found themselves a plot of land almost adjoining their daughter's cottage and with a frontage onto the High Street, just 50 yards or so from the beach. I received the commission to design and build the house. The budget was a substantial one and it was possible to make good use of local limestone in the structure. The roof was slated with thick, random-coursed rustic slates obtained from a small (two-man!) quarry in South Caernarfonshire. The slates were green in colour, unlike the usual dark blue to purple slates quarried in North Wales, the rustic quality being given to the slates by reason of the flecking imparted by a brownish ochre inherent in the slate. Slabs of the same slate were used for areas of external wall claddings.

The Le Mares and the Burns enjoyed their summer houses in Rhosneigr for many years after construction and they became good friends of Dorothy and myself against the background of the rather hectic summer social round of the village.

Pritchard house and shop

In the 1950s, the corner shop was still a viable proposition, to the extent that the shopkeeper was prepared to invest, in suitable places, in the construction of new shops with living accommodation attached. These were interesting commercial, but also one-off house commissions undertaken for fellow small business proprietors who were very conscious that the money was being spent on the new building, firstly to ensure their livelihood and only secondly on a home. Two of the photographs here are of grocer's shops serving an immediate local community, staffed by the patron and his wife, on call from early morning until mid-evening by dint of having their living accommodation adjacent to their working area. The viability of such premises was however, soon to be decimated by the onset of the supermarket.

The third photograph is of an extension to an historic building in Betws-y-Coed providing additional retail space on the ground floor for this Welsh Wool Shop, with living accommodation over. The insertion of this modern shop extension and flat within this sensitive environment posed a difficult design problem.

Welsh Wool Shop and flat

Penri Jones house and shop

Design elevation

Although not the direct concern of any of these projects, but because of their semi-commercial nature, it is appropriate to add here a word or two on the important matter of architect's fees for private house commissions. Described elsewhere in this book is the detailed work undertaken on such commissions by an architect before and after the 'pretty pictures' of the proposed buildings have been completed. In the 1950s and 1960s the RIBA Scale of Charges was obligatory for the architect and, other than for very small projects smaller than a private house, the standard fee for complete services was 6% on the contract sum. This divided, in broad terms, as to 30% up to the approval of design drawings, a further 40% up to the tender stage and the remaining 30% for overseeing the construction phase, issuing certificates for payments to the contractor, ensuring that the work conformed to the drawings and specification and dealing with any problems arising during the six months' maintenance period. The fees were to be paid on completion of each of the first two stages and in tranches during the contract period.

Generally speaking, the fees flowed quite well during the first two stages but, very often, at the end of the contract there were still billed fees awaiting payment. The trouble is that a client can find so many minor things to grumble about as the work progresses towards completion, particularly if the contractor is falling behind programme. There is also the problem of additional fees which might be arising for work which has been carried out which is not covered by the scale fees, such as if revised drawings have to be prepared because of changes in mind on the part of the client during the production drawings or contract periods.

The difficulty for the private architect is that these withheld or disputed fees, even though they may be only the last 10% to 20% of the total fee, represent the profit, and thus the livelihood of the architect after his overheads and staff salaries have been paid. The pursuance of these last tranches of fees can thus often be an exhausting and painful experience - for both architect and client.

Pocklington house

Before moving to Colwyn Bay in 1955 it was necessary to carry out minor alterations and refurbishment to our newly acquired house. We were lucky in finding exactly the right kind of small local builders for that work - the brothers Roberts, both joinery tradesmen working with four or five other tradesmen. The work was carried out in good time and at reasonable cost. At one of my earlier meetings at the house with the Roberts I was told that they had a customer who wished to build a new house in Colwyn Bay and would I be willing to meet them? Of course I would!

The Pocklingtons turned out to be a master miller and his wife from Staffordshire. Mr Pocklington was of retirement age and they had found a small piece of land on which they wished to build the house, using the Roberts brothers for the work. The 'small plot' was, in fact, one of the most desirable sites for a new house in Colwyn Bay. It had been the garden for the Mount Stewart Hotel on the promenade in Rhos-on-Sea, situated across Rhos Road from the hotel, on a corner plot of the

Cayley Promenade. The ground level was raised well above road level and was supported along the road frontages by massive stone squared rubble walling embracing stone flights of steps, linking the gardens to the promenade.

The budget for the house was generous, the emphasis being on the use of good quality materials rather than on the economy of construction. The single-storey house covered most of the small plot area, leaving a square courtyard garden to the rear, bounded on two sides by the wings of the house and on the third by an existing brick and timber pergola. The Rhos Road wing of the house was carried over a double garage excavated out to road level. Rustic green Welsh slate was used for the roof and the walls of the house were largely in stone, echoing the squared rubble of the retaining walls and contrasted with areas of rendered brickwork.

This was all in 1957 - seven years after the commencement of my architectural practice and at a time when some 250 individual commissions had been undertaken, many of them for new dwellings for special clients. The staff of the practice had grown to six, including myself and three other architects or architectural assistants. I was reminded at that time of my first experience with a private architectural practice of about that size.

After the end of the 1939/45 war, I was still in the Royal Navy, anxious to be demobilized as soon as possible to get on with my architectural studies now that the war was over. The Government announced that demobilization priority was to be given to any members of the armed forces who were qualified to assist with the housing drive. It was necessary to have a sponsoring office and my father was a good friend of one William George of Ashton-under-Lyne who, although not a member of the RIBA, was what was termed in those days a Registered Architect under the terms of the Architects Registration Act of 1937, which gave that status to those who were not qualified by examination but who had spent most of their lives in architectural practice. His father before him had founded the practice in the late 19th century and it had a thriving local connection. Mr George said that he could do with an extra pair of hands around the office, the necessary forms were completed and my 'Class B' release duly came through.

I thus became an acting, unpaid, junior architectural assistant to the William George and Son practice for the next several months until I was able to say my farewells and get back to architectural college at the beginning of the next academic year. My companions on the staff, apart from Mr George, were one sex-obsessed architectural assistant, one rather vague structural steelwork draughtsman on loan from a firm of steelwork contractors and one elderly, long-haired bearded gentleman who much preferred his other hat as an eccentric local artist and whose work in the office was mostly the lettering and colouring-up or blueprinting of other people's drawings - and keeping the office fires well stoked. The main work of the practice was the maintenance and extension of one enormous local power station which was being extended in every direction as fast as possible to meet the burgeoning postwar demand for electricity.

A new housing estate for the local authority had just come into the office when I joined them and I was handed a set of drawings for an earlier pre-war local authority estate which had been carried out by the practice in the late 1920s and I was told that those houses would suffice for the new scheme and should simply be re-drawn for the new estate. All attempts at changes or improvements were rejected. Nevertheless the experience was invaluable and my own staff of five in 1956 was rather more suitably composed than the William George collection of eccentrics!

HESITANT PLANNING OFFICERS

Mars Jones house

Mrs Mars Jones was a widow whose childhood home was Llansannan, a village in the heart of the Denbighshire hills, 15 miles to the south of the North Wales coastline. Her nephew was a well known QC and judge on the Chester circuit. She wished to return to Llansannan and had obtained a small plot of land in the village on which she wished to build a modest new dwelling.

Llansannan is a small, remote village set amongst high encircling hills, so that the whole of the village is in view from some distance away on the approach roads. New building in the village was a rarity in those days and I knew the County Planning Officer to be very much of a traditionalist, in contrast to his opposite numbers in Caernarfonshire and Anglesey who were appreciative of good design - whether in a traditional or modern idiom.

The Denbighshire Planning Officer was not an architect-planner and he was inclined to be hesitant over approvals when faced with design proposals which departed from well-tried traditional formulae. A system which operated for hesitant planning officers in North Wales in those days involved a reference to a panel of architects nominated by the President of the North Wales Society of Architects. In practice, such references were considered by those architects present at the monthly meetings of the Council of the Society at the end of their business meetings.

The role of the local planning officers in development control is not an enviable one. No more than about 20% to 30% of the applications they receive for planning permission are submitted by architects. The rest come partly from architectural technicians either working on their own in a private capacity or moonlighting from their daytime jobs on the staff of a large office. Many others are submitted by builders' draughtsmen or even by private individuals themselves, who are inclined to accompany their application with outlines of what they would like to build executed in fountain pen on graph paper. The planning officers have little option but to turn down any significant proposals for development which fail to define the proposals satisfactorily or where design standards are clearly below par, often with a suggestion that the applicant might wish to consult an architect, if the proposals have some inherent merit. Where proposals of this nature came before the architects' panel (sometimes because they had been submitted by, or on behalf of a local councillor) the panel had little difficulty in recommending a rejection of the proposals.

Other references to the panel were however, made by the planning officers where they had been submitted by an architect, perhaps of good reputation, but where the planning officer did not feel that the design, however well thought out and presented, was appropriate for the proposed setting. These were the most difficult schemes for the panel to consider, in some embarrassing cases in the enforced departure from the meeting of the Council member who had made the controversial application. A consensus was however, usually reached, if necessary on a majority vote, and a decision either in favour of approval or rejection would be conveyed to the planning authority.

Rural Denbighshire was unfamiliar territory to me for private house building and, aware of the traditional bias of the County Planning Officer, I was apprehensive that this small house might well be my first planning application to end up in the arms of the NWSA Council at our next meeting. The designs for this house were therefore most conservative. In the event there were indeed long-running problems with the planning authority on the application, but these were because of the desire of the planning officer to change the proposed site for the house entirely, to another part of the village. In the end however, consensus prevailed and the house was built on the planned site, albeit moved in position a little on that site, thus ensuring that honour was sustained all round.

Gysin house, Y Glyn

Extensions to existing dwellings often pose the most difficult domestic design problems, particularly where the original house holds historic interest. The easy approach is perhaps to copy slavishly the building materials and characteristics of the existing dwelling and thus to merge the extension into the whole. The disadvantage here is that this will often destroy the balance and character of the original building which will have been conceived as a balanced composition.

A more difficult choice is to create a sharp contrast for the extension as against the original structure. Handled sensitively, this can enhance the quality of the existing composition, leaving it to make a clear statement of its own, whilst further interest is then added with the differing characteristics of the new extension. The dangers of an unsuccessful marriage and the spoilage of an historic building are however always present, particularly when that building is set within a group of similar historic structures.

Y Glyn is an early 19th century mansion on the mainland shore of the Menai Straits, built well before the railway line and the nearby Britannia Bridge by Stephenson carrying that main line to Holyhead over the Straits. The railway was however, built to pass close by between the coast road and the house, but well below the level of the house. The building of the railway nevertheless involved the diversion of the drive and the building of a bridge to carry the railway over the drive close to the main road lodge.

Y Glyn before part-demolition and renovation

In late Victorian times, the house was extended to well over twice the original size by the addition of substantial new wings on either side of the original house and a grotesque entrance porch. On one side a service wing was built, providing new kitchens, stores and staff accommodation and on the other side, extensions to the living accommodation. These wings were not successful extensions, either from an aesthetic point of view or in the quality of the building work and materials. The Gysin family, from Switzerland, who acquired the estate in the late 1950s had a keen sense of history and architectural character and, having explained their accommodation requirements to me, readily agreed to the complete demolition of the Victorian additions, the renovation and enhancement of the original Georgian core and the construction of extensions to house a new kitchen and garage wing.

No attempt was made to echo the characteristics of the original house in the new extension and this was built in a modest manner reflecting the use of the new wing as a modern kitchen and accommodation for the family cars. On the other hand it was felt that the Georgian facade would benefit from the addition of a new entrance porch and, rather than designing this as a 20th century reproduction of an 18th century porch, I determined to see whether an appropriate original structure could be found and transported to Bangor for addition to the front of Y Glyn.

My first stop was with Bert Crowther, the architectural antique dealer at Syon Lodge in Twickenham who had always been able to find suitable doors and panelling of the correct period for me for use in old houses. 'Crowthers of Syon Lodge' have nowadays acquired cult status, with premises in Bond Street and Pimlico Road as well as at Syon Lodge but, in the 1950s, their stock was bundled haphazardly around the grounds of Syon Lodge in a state of some disarray. Nevertheless Bert would always respond to interest expressed in a particular piece uncovered from one of the heaps by asserting that it was one of his prize possessions with which he would be most reluctant to part, but could perhaps be persuaded to do so by a very special price.

Sure enough, Bert Crowther came up with the perfect Georgian porch in an overgrown corner of the yard looking very dilapidated, but correct in size and character for what I had in mind. After some hard bargaining, including for the safe delivery of the porch over the 250 miles to Bangor, the deal was concluded and the result, after some careful minor renovations, can be seen in the photograph of the house as this was completed for occupation.

Twist house

Mr Twist was a garage and motor showroom owner in Manchester, living in Hale in Cheshire. The Twists chose Llandudno as the place for their second home in Wales. The site they acquired was a precipitous piece of cliff on the Great Orme facing south and lying between the perimeter road and high-water mark. Clearly a problem site.

The Twists were devotees of the South of France and came to my office armed with the usual file of magazine cuttings and lavishly illustrated books of the Côtes de Provence style of domestic architecture. Fortunately their budget was commensurate with the site problems and their ambitions for the house.

The photographs illustrate the manner in which the house was positioned at a level at which the roof of the house was below the road level, resulting in a steeply sloping tortuous drive squeezed into the available space and linking the entrance gates with the garage at first floor level. The treatment of the roof was obviously of some importance, the whole of the area of the roof being in full view every time the house was approached, as well as constituting the only view of the house to be seen from the public roadway. This coincided well with the Côtes de Provence style requirements in that I was able to use rust-coloured Spanish tiles (imported from Belgium!) for the roof to both satisfy the need for a distinctive, attractive roof treatment and the style preferences of the clients.

The detailing of the wrought ironwork, specifically identified by the client and lifted straight from their Côtes de Provence style books is less satisfactory in this North Wales coastal position, but the overall design was well received both by the client and the planning authority. The building contract was not an easy one but we were fortunate in having an excellent bricklayer-trained general foreman on site throughout the contract who was a tower of strength in the day-to-day decisions needed by the architect and contractor to achieve the construction of this uniquely situated house.

Entrance bridge

Whilst working on this Llandudno project for the Twists, I became involved in proposals for the design of a large building in central Manchester on a site on which Mr Twist had an option and where he wanted to construct a new motor showroom with several storeys of offices over. Proposals were prepared for this multi-storey project which were admittedly set at a rather high density of development in order to achieve economic reality for the project. A planning refusal was received on the grounds of excessive density and Mr Twist determined to appeal the decision. That appeal was lodged and a scale model of the proposed building was built. Our client decided that the appeal would be presented by a past-President of the Town Planning Institute and I was asked to visit him at his offices to determine strategy for the public enquiry. An appointment was arranged at his office for 11am on a particular day.

The house from the cliff edge

I arrived at the Planning Consultant's office on the appointed day well armed with the files for the project and ready for several hours of discussion, strategy planning and note-taking ahead of the pending appeal. After a short half-hour of fairly desultory chat about the project however, I was rather startled to be told that it was very nearly lunchtime and that this eminent planner/architect wished to show me a recently completed public house and restaurant which he had designed and built. Off we went to this exhibit, a mile or two out of town - a passable enough building encompassing the public bars and adjoining restaurant, which was not yet open.

Ten or fifteen minutes sufficed for a tour of the accommodation and it was made clear that the waiting time was to be spent in one of the bars. I settled for a glass of sherry but was a little alarmed to hear my companion ordering a large pink gin for himself. A further round followed before the restaurant opened. Presented with the menu I opted for a gammon steak with an egg but, when the head waiter asked my planning consultant colleague for his order he declined food and ordered another large pink gin. Another large pink followed before I had finished my gammon and, anxious to avoid any further additions to the profits of the bar side of the establishment and to get back to the office, I declined further courses or coffee and we left the premises.

I had thought that we would be going straight back to the office to get down to the business of the day, but we embarked on a circuitous route on which several completed building projects of my companion were visited and explained in detail.

As we neared the town centre I again thought that we would shortly be back at the office, but it transpired that that there was urgent business to conclude on the way back at the local Conservative Club which it was hoped I would excuse. The business was, of course, two more large pink gins at the still open bar, even though it was fast approaching four o'clock in the afternoon. Fortunately, the office was only a short (hair-raising!) drive around the corner and we finally arrived back at the office desk shortly before four o'clock.

It was clear that our consultant was now in no fit state to give serious consideration to any matters concerning the showroom appeal and, after a short difficult discussion on general tactics, I made my departure. The subsequent appeal, not particularly surprisingly, was lost.

Motor showroom/office building model

A LATTER-DAY BILL GATES

Fielden house

Jack Fielden was a 1950s equivalent of the 1990s' Bill Gates in America. He founded an electronics research and manufacturing business in Manchester and was at the cutting edge of what would now be regarded as the rather primitive electronics industry in those middle years of the 20th century. To maintain the forward impetus of the business he decided to move the research side of the enterprise to North Wales and he found the ideal property in an Edwardian red brick mansion on the mainland side of the Menai Straits, tucked snugly in the lee of Telford's A5 suspension bridge which spans the Straits close to the house.

To provide living accommodation for himself and his family when in Caernarfonshire my client decided to build himself a new house alongside the mansion laboratories, separated from those buldings only by a narrow lane and trapped between the A5 and the lane. The required single storey house inevitably was going to be a long and thin structure.

The physical limitations of the site were thus quite formidable but, more than this, the prominent position of the house, in an elevated position on the wooded shoreline, made the design solution an important one in the terms of the view of the Caernarfonshire shore from Anglesey and from traffic crossing the Telford suspension bridge from Anglesey to Caernarfonshire.

Duncan Sandys was Minister of Housing and Local Government from 1954 onwards and he sponsored the foundation of the Civic Trust in 1957. One of the early moves of the newly-formed Trust was the establishment of triennial Civic Trust Awards nationwide, with the cities having their round of awards in one year, the counties in the next year and the London area in the third year. The first round of county awards occurred in 1959, but Anglesey did not join in the award scheme for that year. Caernarfonshire did so however, and the just-completed Fielden house was put forward in response to letters from the County Council asking for entries.

Two Civic Trust Awards were awarded in Caernarfonshire in 1959 and the Fielden house was one of those recipients. The plaques for mounting on the building were presented at the next quarterly meeting of the County Council at Shire Hall, Caernarfon. The citations of the assessor for the awards were read out to the assembled County Councillors and when the citation for the Fielden house reached the words, *"this building of contemporary design, eminently suits the landscape, and appears far more happily established than many of its older neighbours which for all time will be foreigners to their setting"* - my fellow architect recipient of an Award (for a tree-planting exercise) who was an elderly local Welsh architect not renowned for his appreciation of modern architecture, laughed out loud. This exhibition of dissent from a fellow architect brought to my mind the title of a book written by Trystan Edwards in 1924 entitled *Good and Bad Manners in Architecture*. The author was, of course, referring to the need for courtesy in architectural design, but this incident was certainly the worst case of actual bad manners I have experienced on the part of a fellow architect. As a young architect close to the beginning of his career, I was most proud of the receipt of this first Civic Trust Award; the sardonic laughter hurt badly and has remained in my memory until this day.

House from the Anglesey shore

The house and the Menai straits

Soon after the Fieldens moved into their new house, Fielden Electronics were awarded a major Government research project, worth £1 million in 1950s' money - say £20 million today - and I was asked to design, construct and have ready for occupation a complete new electronic research laboratory on an Anglesey industrial estate, all within 12 weeks! This was done by combining a mixture of local rubble stonework with standard prefabricated timber walls, roof and floors (and laying the foundations and floor slabs before receiving a planning permission) but that is another story.

Harrison house

This is yet another small holiday house built in Rhosneigr, this time for the Harrison family. They had found a small pocket-handkerchief piece of land which, bounded by two earlier houses close to the crossroads at the top of the High Street, had been overlooked for many years. It became one of my favourite holiday houses: small, compact and having a tiny but well-protected garden. The initial sketch proposals were accepted immediately by the client and the house was completed without undue complications, helped by the fact that the builder's office was just around the corner only a few yards away from the site!

Not all commissions for single, one-off design houses go quite as smoothly as this. A popular image of the work of an architect is that this more or less begins and ends with the production of pretty design sketches which somehow become translated into completed buildings without a great deal of further work on his part. The reality, of course, is that the pretty sketches are the result firstly of the production of detailed survey drawings involving the measurement, in plan and section, of all the physical features of the site and the plotting, by surveying instrument, of the changes in ground level which occur across the site. Many rough sketches will then be prepared and abandoned in endeavours to meet the written brief which is prepared by the architect and endorsed by the client before design work is commenced. The best possible solution for the requirements of the client and the exigencies of the site revealed by the survey information eventually emerge and design drawings are completed. Preliminary estimates of cost are then calculated for that scheme.

Sometimes the client will accept the resulting design drawings, and the budget, without demur, but there will often be the need to produce revised drawings because of opposition by the client to certain features of the proposals or, just as often, to changes of mind on the part of the client over the requirements of the previously endorsed brief. Given approval of the final sketch proposals, the real work of making the building become a reality can be commenced.

A detailed planning permission must be obtained from the planning authority for the construction of the proposals. If the design has taken good account of the immediate environment and is in accord with the requirements of the local authority Development Plan, the required permission will be received, usually between two and three months after making the application, perhaps after some minor adjustments to detail in negotiation with the planning officers. If that good account has not been taken, the required permission could well be badly delayed whilst major changes are sought to the drawings, and, if those changes are not forthcoming, a formal refusal of the application might well be received, not, I am happy to say, a situation in which any of these Special Houses for Special People became embroiled.

Given the receipt of a detailed planning permission, new drawings now need to be prepared, usually to larger scales, which reduce the pretty pictures to terms which can be used by the quantity surveyor and/or the contractor for producing the lists of labour and materials which will be needed to construct and fit out the building and to calculate the cost of doing so.

For a one-off house, three or four contractors who can be relied upon to maintain good standards of craftsmanship will be invited to tender on the basis of drawings, specification and, in the case of larger houses, using the bills of quantities which have been produced by the quantity surveyors. Whilst the tendering process is proceeding, detailed drawings will be deposited with the local building inspectors for what used to be bye-law approval and is now building regulation approval. There are hundreds of different regulations which must be observed in obtaining this approval and building inspectors always seem pleased to be able to find a dozen or so minor ways in which the drawings do not conform, or have not been annotated, to the standard required by the regulations. New and revised submissions are needed to deal with such matters.

Tenders are received and the lowest tender is usually accepted although, if this is over budget, revisions to the drawings and specification may be necessary to bring it back within the required figure. Difficult negotiations with the lowest tenderer are often necessary before this can be achieved. Agreement having been reached however, the form of contract is drawn up by the architect for signature by client and contractor and building work can at last commence.

Breeze Hill estate

Emrys Griffiths was the first building contractor I met in Anglesey, well before opening private practice. He was based in Benllech on the north-east coast of the island and had taken over the running of the business recently from his father, William Griffiths, the founder of the firm - which was now called William Griffiths & Son.

Soon after my office opened for business, Mr Griffiths telephoned to say that his firm wished to build a new office for themselves in Benllech. Would I care to prepare drawings and would I go over to Benllech to look at the site? I readily concurred and soon saw the results as the first new building (as distinct from conversions and extensions to existing buildings) of the foundling practice. The new office was modest in size, extending to only some 500 square feet in area, all on one level. It was designed largely as a blank front façade relieved only by two elements, the first being an entrance door, sidelight and canopy over leaving three-quarters of the façade as undisturbed wall. Across that wall, at high level, were set bronze letters reading, 'WILLIAM GRIFFITHS & SON - CONTRACTORS' occupying the remaining width of the frontage.

The rather stark design was accepted in full detail by the Griffiths and this uncompromising building became a point of interest to passing traffic on the north coastal road of the island. William Griffiths & Son went on to build several of the early houses of the practice and a good relationship was maintained between architect and builder. The office, alas, was demolished in the 1980s to make way for a bank.

In the immediate pre-war days Benllech had been expanding rapidly, but it was well behind the established resorts of Rhosneigr and Trearddur Bay and even Red Wharf Bay, resorts served by the railway lines of the island. Development was slow to resume after the war because of the licensing problems but, as soon as restrictions were removed, Mr Griffiths wished to resume housebuilding on land which the firm had owned since pre-war days. I was appointed to design the houses for an area of land which was (appropriately) to be called Breeze Hill Estate.

Architects were often reluctant to become involved in speculative house-building projects, firstly because the nature of such builders was to be parsimonious over the extent of the fees to be paid to the architect and, even then, only rather late in the day. Just as importantly, a builder was often only really interested in seeing a detailed planning permission obtained for the houses, after which he was inclined to depart in minor ways from positioning, floor plan and elevational detail, perhaps not sufficient to pull down the wrath of the planning authority, but quite sufficient to destroy the integrity of the design concept. In the worst cases, architects have been known to disown any connection with such a completed project and even to make lengthy detours to avoid passing and (once again) becoming appalled by what had arisen from the ground.

By now however, Emrys Griffiths and I had known each other for sufficient time and had worked together long enough to give confidence that what was designed would be built and that there would be continuing co-operation between builder and architect as the work progressed and problems of detail arose. The proposals for the estate of some 40 houses accordingly proceeded and confidence was well rewarded. The groups of single-storey houses were built well and they sold well. Houses were reserved as they were started and, when the first stage had been completed, a convenient Civic Trust Award year arose and Breeze Hill was entered for consideration. The result was one of the very first speculative housing schemes in the United Kingdom to receive a Civic Trust Award and William Griffiths & Son were delighted, not least by the burgeoning demand for their houses which resulted from the Award.

This book is essentially concerned with one-off houses and their owners, but work for builders' housebuilding projects form an essential part of the story of the advance of the Lingard practice (including the design of schemes running to many hundreds of houses during the few years covered by this book) and, here and there, examples of typical houses from such commissions have been slipped into the saga.

Netherclift house

The Bodorgan Estate occupies some 50 square miles of Anglesey, mostly on the south-east corner of the island. The estate is owned by the Meyrick family, whose other land holdings in the UK include a large part of Bournemouth on the south coast of England. The main estate office for the family is in Bournemouth but there is also a subsidiary estate office in Bodorgan in Anglesey. The unspoiled rural character of this area of the island is largely the result of the careful supervision and control of all development, whether agricultural or built, by the Bodorgan estate office.

That estate office had commissioned me to undertake improvement grant work in respect of a number of the farmhouses and cottages on the estate and my contact with the estate for that work was with Mr Milligan, the then Assistant Land Agent in the Bodorgan office. The Chief Agent for the estate in Anglesey was Mr Netherclift who was, at that time, approaching retirement age.

I heard from the Netherclifts shortly before that retirement date to say that they had negotiated the acquisition of a plot of land from the estate on which they wished to build their retirement home. The land was in a fine position on a ridge looking out to the mountains of Snowdonia and overlooking the waters of the Malltraeth Estuary, an estuary which has been immortalised by Charles Tunnicliffe RA in his studies of the bird life of the estuary.

This single-storey house was sturdily built, using Welsh slate for the roof and local stone for much of the external walling - as befitted the exposed nature of the site. An architectural affectation which may not be apparent from the photograph was that, although a window in the stone, west gable wall of the garage was not wanted by the clients, I felt that an unbroken area of stonework in this prominent position was undesirable and I persuaded the clients to accept a deepset window opening, with timber frame and sawn slate sill, but glazed with black vitrolite, completely obscure glass, to provide the required point of interest in the composition. The house was ready for the Netherclifts to move into on their retirement, just a few hundred yards away from the Bodorgan Estate office, where Mr Milligan took over the reins of management, although he was soon to move to Bournemouth as Chief Agent for the whole of the Meyrick empire.

The part played by the great estates in the conservation of the traditional environment and in the control of development on their land is often greatly underestimated. Our Town and Country Planning system, of course, has had an important part to play in this matter since the 1940s, but that role can be described, in cricketing terms, as being something of a long-stop. The planners do their best to encourage good development, but their role is essentially a negative one of acceptance or refusal and they have few powers to initiate and create detailed developments of character and quality. On the other hand, some of our finest residential and holiday complexes have been planned and developed, and then nurtured, by our great estates.

As noted earlier, the Meyrick family have been responsible over many generations for both the preservation of the rural ecology in southern Anglesey and, at the same time, the development of what is probably the finest example of a planned holiday and residential resort in the country in Bournemouth. Similarly the Mostyn family have been responsible for the creation and protection of Llandudno, arguably one of the finest seaside promenades in Europe, still limited to hotels on the sea frontage, with commercial development confined solely to the hinterland behind the magnificent sweep of the promenade. Lord Street in Southport, created by the Hesketh family is without doubt the finest example of a resort core in the North of England; and the Grosvenors, in overseeing much of the development and protection of the historic core of Chester, the whole of Belgravia and parts of Pimlico and Mayfair in London, have created and preserved work in built environments of exceptional quality and character.

There are many other such instances, but a more recent example of a controlled holiday development of exceptional quality, created and overseen for several generations by one man is Portmerion in Wales. Now handed over to a trust for preservation for future generations this creation of the late Sir Clough Williams Ellis is without parallel. All achieved without a jot of assistance from a planning authority. Indeed, I can recollect the indignation of Sir Clough one day late in his long life when he told me about a request he had received from a local planning office assistant for the repositioning of a small window he had introduced, without permission, into one of the village cottages.

Ducksbury house

Mr and Mrs Ducksbury owned and ran the George Hotel in Huddersfield, an oasis of good living in an area not notably renowned for fine cuisine and comfortable hotels in the 1950s. For their relaxation periods from the stress of the hotel business, they retreated to a cottage near the eastern tip of Anglesey. As retirement neared for Mr Ducksbury, they decided to build themselves a larger house in Anglesey and they were fortunate in locating a piece of land enjoying beach frontage on the shore between Beaumaris and Penmon. I have referred more than once to the magnificent views which many sites in Anglesey enjoy of the coastline, the Menai Straits and the mountains beyond, but the Ducksbury site arguably outshone all the others. The prospect is out across the sea at the point where the Menai Straits widen out to become Conwy Bay, with the nearest point of the Caernarfonshire shore being some two or three miles away. That shoreline is edged by the precipitous slopes of the heather-covered Penmaenmawr mountain rising to some 2,000 feet above sea level and framing the view of the Conwy estuary,

Deganwy and the Llandudno West Shore five miles away across the bay. Towards the left-hand side of the view the Great Orme rises out of the sea, exposing the whole of the two-mile long south-western flank of that massive rock to this part of Anglesey. To the north of the Orme the open Irish Sea is then to be glimpsed framed by the outline of Puffin Island. All in all a truly memorable situation for a new house.

The immediate background to the house is low-lying and it was agreed by the clients that we should keep the profile of the house low to ensure as little intrusion as possible into this otherwise idyllic scene. At the same time, in order to bring the magnificent view into the living areas of the house, the south-east elevation was to be almost entirely glazed.

The word 'compromise' has been used occasionally about earlier houses in relation to endeavours to relate clients' requirements and preferences to the honest use of building materials and the 'fitness for purpose' of the completed structure, but here was one commission where no such even minor compromise was necessary. The result was, I believe, one of the first of these early houses which the practice could claim to be truly faithful to the principles of the modern movement in architecture.

One conflict which did arise in this concept of a truly modern house was that, when first visiting the Ducksburys in their Anglesey cottage, it was notable that there was a huge log fire burning in the *cwm fawr* - the traditional cottage hearth, despite the fact that it was early in the summer months. Part of the need for a fire of that nature was that the cottage had no central heating and the thick stone walls and traditional small windows meant that the structure was slow to warm up in response to the strengthening rays of the sun; but the open fire obviously also formed an important part of the lives of the couple.

The main form of heating for the new house was to be underfloor electric wiring enabling the floor slab to be heated during the night at cheap rates for the electricity, leaving the stored heat in the slab to be dispersed into the house progressively over the subsequent 15 hours or so.

Sure enough however, the brief for the house carried a stipulation that an open fire was to be provided in the sitting room and dining area. This posed a problem because, with a single-storied, flat-roofed house the rise from the hearth to the roof level was barely eight feet and, because of the low profile taken by the structure, only a foot or two was possible for the additional height of the chimney. Because the fire was required to be visible from separate areas of the house, the design for the hearth was one of a free-standing fire, open on three sides with a ducted external air ventilation grid below and a copper hood above to carry the draught from the vent up into the brickwork of the flue. Despite also the provision of a special chimney pot to increase the upward movement of air in the chimney, there was insufficient draught to prevent the fire smoking in even quite moderate winds. Much experimentation followed, with a new, lower hood being introduced to capture the smoke and, when that failed to completely solve the problem, the introduction of armour-plate, heatproof glass to two sides of the open fire - which did the trick. Smoking ceased and honour was restored!

From the shore

Paraphrased from his play *The Birds*, Aristophanes had this to say on this very matter:

> To talk of architecture is a joke
> Till you can build a chimney which won't smoke.

The playwright seemingly had encountered similar persistent problems some two and a half thousand years previously!

Soon after completion of the Ducksbury house, I was approached by a director of Pochins, a Cheshire firm of contractors who were very active in North Wales, to say that he had acquired the companion site to the Ducksbury house on the other side of the lane leading to the shore and enjoying exactly the same views and shore frontage as that house.

Being a director of a building firm, Mr Broadbent only required design services for his house and, at the end of the day, there were some minor departures from the original concept, but nevertheless a fine house was erected for this wonderful position.

My stark recollection of the period when the Broadbents were building their house was when I received a telephone call from Mr Broadbent one Friday asking me to telephone back to discuss some detail or other of the design. I did not telephone back until the following Monday morning, to be told by his office that he was in hospital receiving treatment for serious injuries sustained late on the Friday afternoon. Apparently he had taken delivery that afternoon of a brand new Jaguar motor car and, on the way home had driven out from a minor road to cross the new Northwich by-pass, when he was hit by another vehicle travelling at high speed along the dual carriageway.

Mr Broadbent recovered from his injuries in due course but the Jaguar was a complete write-off on the first day out of the showroom with only a handful of miles on the mileometer.

COMMODITY, FIRMNESS AND DELIGHT

Richards house

The words of Henry Wotton in his book *The Elements of Architecture* (1624) in defining the requirements for good architecture and fine building, are still as relevant today as they were in the early 17th century:

> In architecture as in all other operative arts, the end must direct the operation. The end is to build well. Well building hath three conditions. Commodity, Firmness and Delight.

These three all-embracing principles were in fact first set down by Vitruvius in his treatise *De Architectura* written in the 1st century AD. Firmness is usually taken as being sound structural design for the building but the firmness of a building also means firmness of detail to ensure that moisture does not penetrate through to, or gather within, the interior.

Commodity is the fitness of the building for the purpose intended. Is everything properly provided for within the building shell; can the most common tasks be carried out with the the minimum of movement; are the internal details designed to avoid personal injury; are there adequate storage provisions in the right places; do the rooms accommodate satisfactorily the loose furniture required for the particular spaces; is there enough, and not too much, natural light and sunlight evident where it is needed and conducive to the well-being of the occupants; is there a good relationship between the indoor and outdoor spaces; do the heating, electrical and ventilation systems deliver adequate and adaptable warmth, artificial light and fresh air to the dwelling; does the fabric of the building ensure that no more fuel than is necessary is expended on creating and maintaining comfortable conditions in the winter months and in keeping the interior cool in the summer months; are annual maintenance costs for the building structure as low as possible? There are no doubt many other factors which can be added to this list.

Sometimes these essential requirements for a successful piece of architecture act against each other. This Anglesey house on the edge of a small rocky inlet with a small, pretty beach called Bull Bay was built for Mr Richards and his wife as an early retirement home. Mr Richards had very positive views on creating a house which would need a minimum of external maintenance work. He would thus have no truck with whitened walls which would require repainting every few years, but required to have the rendered walls dashed with self-cleansing shiny small pebbles. More seriously he wished to ensure that no timber was used to the verges and eaves of the roof to avoid the regular treatment of these timbers which would otherwise be needed.

In Anglesey, this latter requirement was at odds with the requirement to protect the external walls by extending the roof over the verges and eaves, and thus the wall cavities and inner lining walls, from the winter gales from the sea and the associated wind-blown rainfall. Projecting eaves and verges finished with bargeboards and fascias protect the upper parts of external walls susceptible to wind-blown rain, and reduce appreciably the chances of rainwater passing across the external wall cavity, to appear as dampness on the inner skin of the external walls. Pointed verges, where the roof slates can only overlap the gable walls by a matter of an inch or so, and eaves where the slating discharges rainwater into the gutters hard up against the external wall face are particularly susceptible to such penetration.

The stipulations of Mr Richards thus lessened the likelihood of Firmness for the house, although improving Commodity by dint of reduced external painting costs. In the view of his architect, the element of Delight in the final appearance of the house was certainly depreciated with the omission of the brim of the hat and the eyebrows for the building.

Tongue house - Parlwr Cottage

Long before the railway line touched the shore near Rhosneigr in the 1840s and became instrumental in the creation of the present holiday village, there was a fisherman's cottage on the lonely shore of a small bay situated at the end of the mile long beach of Traeth Llydan - now known as Broad Beach to the predominantly English holiday residents. The little bay was known as Traeth Parlwr because of the small Braich-y-Parlwr headland which marked one side of the bay and the cottage thus became known as Parlwr Cottage.

The cottage was occupied by the same family through the 19th century and the first half of the 20th century, the incumbent for the dwelling from the 1890s being one Johnny Jones, a well-known local eccentric in the village. He met his death by drowning in the 1950s whilst collecting driftwood on the beach during a violent night-time storm. His story is told in *Rhosneigr - Then and Now* by T T M Hale (Hedgerow Publishing 1990). The rather tumbledown cottage was bought by the Tongue family from Sale in Cheshire and I was asked to prepare proposals for the conversion and renovation of the cottage for family holiday use.

There was a small stone jetty below the house, with the foot of the wall presently well above the high-water mark of the spring tides. This was because the beach of the bay varied much in contour from year to year as the sea was wont to break through the shingle bank linking Braich-y-Parlwr with the mainland in rough weather and high tides, moving many hundreds of tons of sand and shingle out of, or back into, the bay overnight. There was an opportunity here to relate the cottage more closely to the maritime position through utilising traditional limewash whitening and black pitch on the jetty, rock faces, bollards and supporting stone walls to good effect.

Although it was appreciated that these applications would require freshening up every two or three years because of the batterings received from gales or sea-spray, my clients readily agreed to this treatment, sensing the *Delight* that this could afford to themselves and others over the years.

When the next round of Civic Trust Awards came about in 1962 the Anglesey County Council did join the national scheme and Parlwr Cottage was awarded one of the first Civic Trust Awards for Anglesey which followed upon the Fielden House and Breeze Hill estate awards, to give the practice their third Civic Trust Award in three years.

The steps to the beach

This book is concerned mainly with newly built 'special houses for special people' but, where an existing cottage or farmhouse has been completely renovated and has, in effect, become a completely new dwelling, as here with Parlwr Cottage, the house has been included.

What has not been included from these first ten years or so of private practice are any of the many scores of houses where only minor alterations or extensions were designed and implemented by the practice. In many of these cases, the project comprised the equipping of the dwelling with basic amenities through the Improvement Grant system - the provision of running water, hot water systems, modern kitchens and bathrooms, drainage and electric light and power. There were very many dwellings in Anglesey in the 1950s which possessed none of these amenities and trade was very brisk in Improvement Grant applications once it became known that half of the cost of modernisation would be paid for by the local authority.

The wild Rhosneigr shore

One Improvement Grant applicant who has remained vividly in my mind arrived at my office in Llangefni on a Wednesday afternoon, following the morning cattle market in the town. Rubber-booted, tweeded and ruddy-faced, here was clearly a farmhouse Improvement Grant client. A visit to the farm in a remote corner of the island was arranged for the following week and the private lane up to the farm revealed a fine herd of Welsh Black cattle in the fields on either side of the lane. The farmhouse was substantial and there was a brand new Rover motor car parked in the open barn.

There was obviously adequate space within the house to accommodate the new kitchen and bathroom and the location for each was quickly established. I sketched out the proposed floor plans on the spot and, within the bathroom, I pencilled in the proposed positions for the wash-basin, bath and lavatory for approval.

There was a moment's silence and the rather startling conversation which ensued went something like this:-

Client: There's impossible it is. We will not be having that
                filthy thing in the house..

He indicated the loo sketched on plan in the bathroom. It was then my turn for a moment's silence. Thinking that a separate wc on the ground floor off the back porch might be in mind, I said that I doubted whether that would be acceptable for Improvement Grant purposes.

Client: Not by the back door either; there be plenty of fields
                around the house.

It took me another half-an-hour to convince my client that if he wished to take advantage of the Improvement Grant arrangements he was saddled (if that is the correct word) with a water-closet and the eventual solution was to adopt my suggestion of a downstairs lavatory by the back door, with all the plumbing to be provided for the bathroom loo to fulfill the terms of the Grant, but with the pipes sealed off to await the pan and cistern at some future date when his family tired of venturing outside in response to calls of nature during the night.

But that was all probably some time away as the back door arrangements were obviously going to be a distinct improvement on excursions into the fields. Rural Anglesey was indeed still a primitive place in those immediate post-war years.

Rogers house

The tourist industry in the Anglesey of the 1950s was very much the Cinderella of the island economy. Agriculture still held pride of place, with other industries holding little importance and with tourism close to the bottom of the list. The only major tourist operation was centred on Holyhead where the main line trains arrived to meet the packet-boat sailings from Dublin twice a day. This provided a year-round hotel business for the town for transient passengers between sea and rail. Air travel between London and Dublin eliminated the cream of that trade during the 1950s and the remaining Irish Mail trains which thundered non-stop through North Wales in the night, to and from Holyhead, effectively by-passed the island economy.

Early in the 1950s there was an announcement in the local paper that a tourist association was to be founded in Anglesey and that all interested parties were invited to an inaugural meeting in the Bull Hotel in Llangefni, to be chaired by the Clerk to the County Council. As this was only a few steps away from my office, I looked in on the meeting at the appropriate time. It was attended by 20 or 30 local hoteliers, landowners and shopkeepers. The dearth of interest in the well-being of the growing tourist industry on the island was deprecated by the meeting and there was much enthusiasm for the foundation of the new association. Lord Anglesey was elected President, a prominent County Councillor was elected Chairman and, to my astonishment, I found myself elected Hon. Treasurer of the foundling association - an honorary post which I was to hold for the next 20 years or so.

Commissions continued to flow in for individual private houses in the seaside village of Trearddur Bay during the latter half of the 1950s - most of them *maisons de vaçances*. Some of these houses have been featured in this book for separate review but there were too many dwellings, some of them not over-distinguished, for each one to be the subject of individual vignettes. Four, typical of this series of houses, are illustrated here out of the ten further houses designed and built for individual clients in Trearddur Bay between mid-1956 and late 1959.

The roll call for these houses reads as Barton, Hobbins, Bamford, Dyson, Henderson, Preston, Rogers, King, Slater and Harvey. The houses illustrated here are those of Mesdames Dyson and Orton, Mr and Mrs Rogers, Dr King and the Henderson family. Trearddur Bay was undoubtedly the most popular village in Anglesey for building new holiday houses in the post-war years, as it had been in the earlier years of the century. My favourite house from those earlier years was the dour, stone-built house growing out of its own rocky peninsula and connected to the shore by a narrow sea-girt lane. It was reputed that a good deal of *The Cruel Sea* by Nicholas Monsarrat was written at this maritime dwelling where, on a stormy day at high-tide, the sea-spray could be seen to be cascading over the roof of the house.

The Cruel Sea house

Henderson house

Trearddur Bay village is situated on the narrow central neck of Holy Island with the Irish Sea on one side and, only a few hundred yards to the east, the sea water Straits dividing Holy Island from Anglesey itself. Along the Irish Sea side of the island, apart from the main, wide, sandy beach, there are numerous small rocky coves and tiny bays providing idyllic sites for holiday residences, still within the boundaries of this scattered village.

Dr King House

In the late 1950s most of the above new houses were built for between £4,000 and £5,000 and, in the open, windswept character of this rocky coastline the emphasis needed to be on an appropriate degree of modesty for the completed dwelling, a structure which would knit itself into the rocks and heather of the land and seascape rather than being an expression of the individuality of the client (or prima donna architect!), as can so often occur in the design of a single, specially built dwelling. Local rubble stonework, white rendering, low pitch slate or Hardrow slab roofs and white or simply stained woodwork became something of the norm for these Trearddur Bay houses. Hardrow was a heavy concrete slate which had the character of a Cotswold stone slab. It had an irregular outline as distinct from the mechanical correctness of a Marley or Redland concrete slate and, in the light brown colour, it echoed the patina of the local stone. These slates were capable of being laid at lower slopes than natural slate and they also had the advantage of being half the price of Penrhyn slate, which was most helpful for tight house-building budgets.

The main difficulty of relating these new dwellings to Anglesey vernacular building was that, although the external walling materials could follow the traditions of the island, that tradition was also one of tiny sash windows set in the thick stone walls, keeping the weather out of the house and the heat from the single hearth inside the dwelling. In the postwar years, with central heating of the house a standard requirement, the demand was for the extensive use of glass forming whole areas of external wall, particularly where there were magnificent coastal and sea views to be brought into the living areas.

This was a difficult design problem, but the contrasting of large plain surfaces, including the large glass areas, with no hint of quaintness in the detailing, was all essential if the new house was to sit comfortably in the open, sea-washed landscape of Trearddur Bay. A client-imported Victorian street lamp, rescued from his native English town and mounted conspicuously in the drive of what otherwise was an understated house, built in the local vernacular, has been known to reduce such a composition to ridicule - and the architect to tears!

Dyson/Orton house

94

Albinson house

This house for the Albinsons in Glyn Garth was much in the mould of the earlier Ducksbury house. The plot was approached from the coast road up a narrow lane, the ground rising away from the lane towards the north-west, creating a fine site for the house at the top of the plot and giving good views across the Menai Straits. The clients had seen the Ducksbury house and liked the style. The fine prospect, although not as spectacular as for that house, and the similar orientation, ensured that the houses had many similar characteristics. The Albinson house was smaller but the result was an uncompromised example of modern domestic architecture of the 1950s. I was encouraged, at about that time, by a visit to the office by members of senior staff from the School of Architecture in Manchester who, on seeing this house, asked for copies of the drawings to use as an example for their students of a postwar small house designed and built in the contemporary idiom. Of course, the 'example' intended may have been one of 'What Not To Do!'

In my student days in the 1940s, I had always regarded modern architecture as being free from political affiliations. One of the most influential architectural books at that time was F R S Yorke's *The Modern House in England* which brought together some 50 or so private houses which had been built by modern movement architects in the immediate pre-war years. Up to 1939 there had been very few modern buildings built other than for these few private houses and, if there was any conclusion to be drawn from the houses featured in this influential book it was that modern domestic architecture in the 1930s was the preserve of quite wealthy individuals.

As a counter-balance, in the late 1930s, there had been an influx of mostly left-wing-inclined European architects escaping from the totalitarianism of the political extremes and they were responsible for many of the early, significant, modern non-domestic buildings in England such as the Bexhill Pavilion by Chermayeff, the Finsbury Health Centre by the Tecton Partnership, Highpoint Flats in Highgate by Lubetkin and the Impington Village College in Cambridgeshire by Gropius, all of which had a major influence on architectural thinking in the late 1930s; but then all new building was brought to a shuddering halt by the declaration of war in September 1939.

Even after the end of the war in 1945, private building projects of any kind were severely restricted for a further ten years or so, retarding the progress of modern architecture in the private sector in all by over 15 years. Concentration in the immediate postwar years was upon local authority housing, schools and other projects in the public sphere. As light relief, the Attlee Government sponsored the 1951 Festival of Britain which was overseen by Hugh Casson and designed and built entirely by modern movement architects such as Powell and Moya, Ralph Tubbs and H T Cadbury Brown, whose political persuasions covered the full range of the political spectrum. Nevertheless, the 1951 Festival of Britain was seen by the public as being a manifestation of the Socialist Government.

All this ensured that modern architecture came to be directly related to socialism in those years in the public mind. In the pre-war years architectural private practice had been very much a gentleman's occupation, many of the practitioners having come up through the pupilage system which firstly involved matriculation, usually at a fee-paying school, and then the payment of a substantial premium to a private architect for the privilege of working in his office for five years without any chance of changing offices during that period, and all for little, or even no, salary. In the postwar years however, the doors of the profession were opened to less fortunate individuals through state-assisted further education and, as the older practitioners retired, the bent of the profession turned towards the left.

The RIBA and the architectural press followed this trend to the left and, in the first few decades after the war the, at first, mistaken view of the public that socialism and modern architecture walked hand in hand proved to be self-fulfilling. There is however, absolutely no reason why this should be so. Firmness, commodity and delight and fitness for purpose in building, the essential premises of modern architecture, are universal in their application, whether for a National Health hospital or a BUPA hospital, for a private house or public subsidized housing, for a public school or a comprehensive school.

Time will no doubt weaken the associations between left-wing politics and modern architecture, although the 'cronyism' to be observed between our current Labour Government and influential, left-inclined, private architects does nothing to assist in severing the association in the public mind.

Gorst estate - Llandrillo-yn-Rhos

Colwyn Bay was founded by the Cayley family at the time when the railway line along the coast first touched the open seashore in that area in the 1840s. Over the next hundred years the population of the resort, sprawling out over the shoreland of the Cayley estate, rose to some 20,000 souls. The resort thrived, with the railway bringing in hundreds of thousands of visitors each year, from families on a week or a fortnight annual holiday in the hotels and boarding houses to day trippers from Liverpool and Manchester enjoying a day on the piers and sandy beaches which lay within five minutes' walking distance of the station.

By 1939, most of the land of the estate which was not within the flood plain left by the original estuary of the Conwy river, dividing Denbighshire from Caernarfonshire and Rhos-on-Sea from Penrhyn Bay, had been developed. The remaining land was owned by the Wilde family who lived at Odstone, the last house on the Colwyn Bay/Rhos-on-Sea promenade, just before the still extant toll point on this coastal link between Colwyn Bay and Llandudno. A notable feature of this house was a stone plaque on the sea-side boundary wall of the house which stated that this was the point on the shore of the Conwy river from which Celtic sailors embarked on their voyage of discovery to America, which would have pre-dated the Columbus trip by 300 years! Truly a special house for special people', but not one which I had designed, although I did add an elevated sun lounge onto the rear of the house for the Wildes.

Little Orme horizon

The Wildes also owned areas of land in south-east Anglesey and were thus familiar with my work in that area of Wales. In so far as the remaining developable areas of the Cayley estate were concerned, Victor Wilde was reluctant to release the majority of this land for development as it lay in close proximity to Odstone.

One day in 1960 however, I received a call from Tony Gorst, the son partner in Eldon Gorst and Son of Abergele, who asked if I would meet him and his father at their office on the following day. I was able to go as requested and was surprised to be offered an appointment as their architect for the development, for residential purposes, of many acres of the remaining Cayley estate lands, clustered around the ancient Llandrillo-yn-Rhos church and lying between the church and Odstone. The purpose of the proposed development was the construction of some 60 or 70 small single-storey houses for the increasing numbers of retired couples who were arriving to see out their days by the seaside in Colwyn Bay/Rhos-on-Sea.

It was only some time later that I discovered that it was on condition that I was appointed as architect for the development that Victor Wilde had agreed to the sale of the land to the Gorsts.

Whilst again, this work for a speculative house builder does not sit easily with the single houses designed and built for private individuals which are the main subject of this book, nevertheless the fact that the layout and all the house designs were subject to detailed approval by the vendor of the land - who had insisted on my appointment as architect - gave me an unusual degree of control over what was built, and the result was one of the more successful speculative housing estates which stemmed from the practice. Two of the house types designed for the estate are illustrated here.

Peter Hughes house

Peter Hughes was a meteorologist. When it was time to build himself a new house where else should this be but in Dolwyddelan! The rainfall in those parts, amongst the mountains, averages 100 inches a year compared with some 30 inches a year only 20 miles away down by the coast. Snow comes early to Dolwyddelan and, just beyond the village, the road over the mountains to Blaenau Ffestiniog is blocked with snow for many days each year, the piercing wind from the north or east whipping the snow into five or six feet deep drifts, making travel over what is known locally as the Crimea Pass quite impossible. Where else indeed for a meteorologist to pitch his tent!

Mr Hughes was unmarried, living with his mother, and the accommodation they required was untypical for a new dwelling, each of them having their own interests, and occupying largely separate suites of rooms. Their one-acre site lay towards the edge of the village, dominated by Rowen Mountain, rising for 2,000 feet above and away from the village to the east.

Virtually every house in the village was roofed in local slate obtained from the next town over the mountains, Blaenau Ffestiniog. This was obviously a must for the Hughes' roof and was, in any case, obligatory from the point of view of the local planning authority. The difficulty is that natural slate cannot be laid on roofs at an angle of less then 30 degrees and, in a place with the rainfall of Dolwyddelan, the angle should be over 35 degrees to be sure that there is no penetration of wind-blown rain under the slates. A roof of that steepness was not compatible with the type of house which comprised the brief for the commission or the character of this large relatively isolated site. It occurred to me that we might well be able to fulfil the requirements of the planning authority for a slate-covered roof whilst keeping the roof pitch down to a modest angle. The specification adopted for the roof and annotated on the design drawings used for the planning application was for a bitumen-felted roof with small slates laid tile fashion in the hot bitumen as a top layer. No doubt this innovation caused some head-scratching in the office of the planning authority, but the chief planning officer was not unsympathetic to modern architectural solutions and appreciated that the specification fulfilled the politically-based condition of using natural local slate for the roof. The planning permission thus appeared without undue delay.

In an earlier anecdote (33 - Pretty Pictures) the work of a private house architect up to the commencement of a contract is described, but then the task of ensuring that the house is built to accord with the drawing and specifications, and is built well, commences. The contract opens with a site meeting between architect and contractor, usually following the setting out of the building at ground level. The contractor is reminded of his obligations to produce a progress chart for approval which will ensure, if followed, that the contract will be completed by the appointed date. Regular site meetings with the contractor, accompanied by the representatives of sub-contractors at appropriate times, are then held and minuted; the first of these will be when the foundation excavations are complete and ready for inspection and approval. This is usually the time for the client to telephone to say that there must be some mistake as the foundation trenches are enclosing a building shape which is far, far smaller than has been agreed in the design drawings. Always however, an optical illusion.

The house in the landscape

The entrance front

Generally speaking, contact with the client is fairly amicable during the early part of the contract period; final details for the fittings, electrical layout, decoration, etc are settled and instructions on those matters are passed through to the contractor but, once the roof is on and the internal finishes are commenced, so the lists of matters which the client believes should be corrected, varied or replaced can grow week by week. A meeting on site with a client building a house for his own occupation towards the end of the contract can often extend to several hours and produce 30 or 40 items requiring the attention of the architect on his return to the office.

It is now that the chance of a serious dispute between client and architect can occur. Such disputes are usually resolved by the end of the contract when the last licks of paint are being applied, the landscape works are taking effect and the accumulated debris of the building operations are being removed. The client, for the first time, then sees his new home in the form envisaged in the original pretty sketches.

There is still the builder's final account to receive, to consider, to negotiate upon and to approve before submission to the client. The six-months' maintenance period in which defects arising during that time must be scheduled and remedied by the contractor. After which the final certificate can at last be issued, perhaps two years or more after the client first came into the architect's office.

Peter Hughes took an intense interest in both the evolution of the design for the house and the construction period. There were, as always, some second thoughts on detail as the work progressed and as a result there were a number of 'variation orders' issued to the contractor. These variation orders are often a source of controversy at the stage when the contractor's final account is received as they usually involve work which has not been included in the contract sum. If a bill of quantities has been prepared for the tender and contract purposes, as in the case of the Peter Hughes' house, the pricing of the variation orders must bear a correct relationship to the rates for similar work to be found in the contract sum but, very often, there is no such similar work to be found in the contract bills and agreement on an appropriate figure for the work is much more difficult. Small single houses are very often built without the aid of a bill of quantities, using the drawings and specifications only for the pricing of the work. The pricing of variations is then likely to be the subject of much argument, firstly between architect and contractor and then between client and architect over what has been agreed with the contractor. It is therefore wise to know your contractor well before embarking upon a drawings and specification only contract of any size.

Despite a number of variations which occurred during this Peter Hughes' contract, the contractor was one with whom I had worked for many years and, with the benefit of the original bill of quantities, the final account discussions, although quite heated at times were, in the end, amicably resolved to the satisfaction of both contractor and client.

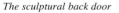
The sculptural back door

The Earlam and Cowham houses

A client name which crops up a good deal in my files for the practice is John Bibby. He was a Liverpool merchant who had a passion for buying up significant properties in North Wales and then seeking my advice on how to develop them. He was sympathetic towards proposals which sought to respect the character of existing buildings, the spaces around those buildings and the associated grounds.

Ravenspoint was built as a large private house in the early years of the 20th century on the cliffs on the southern edge of Trearddur Bay by Sir Harry Grayson for his family of 12 children. The grounds were enclosed on the land side by a two-metre high stone wall marking the perimeter of the several acres of grounds. There was a sea frontage to the site running along the rocky shore at the foot of the cliffs. The house became an exclusive private hotel in later years and was bought as such, including the grounds, by John Bibby in the late 1950s.

I was asked to prepare proposals for the use of the grounds partly for private holiday cottages and, along the sea frontage, more substantial dwellings. Apart from obtaining planning permission for the 20 or so houses to be constructed on the site, the brief included for a contract to construct the roads and services to the plots for the cottages and for the plots to be sold to individuals who wished to build their own houses on the estate. These photographs show the first two houses to be constructed to the individual requirements of the Earlam and Cowham families, the former family comprising the younger end of a well-known Liverpool shipping firm. Behind these two houses, which enjoyed uninterrupted sea views, lay the smaller holiday cottage plots for which I was commissioned by John Bibby to design standard repetitive proposals for two groups of dwellings, one of these groups being glimpsed in the background of the second photograph. The remaining six or seven larger, sea frontage plots were developed one by one for individual clients, some of which are featured in later photographs and essays.

Here again, this group of houses, some of which were built for sale by a local builder, have been included because of the example which can be set by a landowner who has rather more in mind as a developer than the maximizing of early profit at the expense of the environment. It may be a little more expensive to commission an architect for full and individual design services which become part of the contracts for the sale of the plots, but the results can prove to be much more interesting than estates built from drawings taken from a builder's book of plans - and often providing a greater profit to the landowner in the long run.

The Cowham house and the cottage group

It was about this time in the late 1950s that, with a staff of 15, spread between three offices - in Colwyn Bay, Anglesey and Caernarfon - I was desperate to maintain closer touch with the offices when on often lengthy drives to see building sites and clients across the 5,000 square miles or so of North Wales which was covered by the practice. I discovered that if I rented an exclusive fixed telephone landline from my Colwyn Bay office to the 650 feet high top of the Great Orme in Llandudno (where there was a café building) and could persuade the owner to let me mount a transmitter aerial on the roof at the end of the telephone line, I could talk to my office by way of a transmitter/receiver in my car all the way down the coast from Prestatyn to Caernarfon and across most of Anglesey. I was thus able to spend the first three-quarters of an hour of my journeys away from the office going through the morning's mail and dictating responses to a secretary, to be ready for signature and despatch on my return later in the day. I was even able to rig up a way of taking incoming telephone calls to the office into the system (which was strictly illegal) and dealing with those calls from the car. All this some 20 years or more before even the first commercial, limited-cover, car phones appeared on the market.

METAL AND WOOD

Poppleton houses

The Poppletons had a small factory in Colwyn Bay manufacturing metal ducting for artificial ventilation and air-conditioning systems and other sheet metal products. They were an invaluable firm of specialist manufacturers and suppliers for this small but increasingly important part of the building construction process. During the 1960s I received many commissions for the design and fitting out of hotels, restaurants, cafés and coffee bars and the electric fans, ducting and external exhausts, many supplied by Poppletons, formed a vital element in ensuring a comfortable internal environment for these establishments, especially where the cooking and serving arrangements were within the public area and not confined in kitchens to the rear of the premises. The Poppletons provided an excellent service of advice, design and construction for such ventilation systems and, furthermore, always managed to deliver and complete on time on what were invariably contract periods which were far too short in the impatient catering world.

In the pre-war days Colwyn Bay was largely contained within a relatively narrow strip along the shoreline because of the steeply wooded slopes which divided the developed area from the high moorland plateau which lay above the woodland. There was, and is still, only one steep winding main road leading out of the town centre to the south, there to continue on along the high moorland road to Llanrwst.

A few large houses (whose occupants owned motor cars giving them easy access to the town centre) had been built along the ridge line in pre-war days, enjoying fine views of the Conwy Valley and across the valley to the Caernarfonshire mountains beyond. An 18-hole golf course occupied a good deal of the land immediately above the woodland area. With the arrival of the family car in the postwar years, Colwyn Bay exploded into the high land and many hundreds of houses were built in Upper Colwyn Bay during and after the 1960s, swallowing up the golf course on their way up the hills.

The Poppletons acquired a site bounding the Llanrwst Road, just large enough to take two dwellings and these were to be designed as a pair of semi-detached houses for two separate branches of the family. Having their own extensive contacts amongst builders and other sub-contractors, they undertook responsibility for the building contract themselves and I did not therefore become involved in the interior detailing of what were probably the best-ventilated domestic kitchens in Wales!

Whilst on the subject of sub-contractors it should be emphasized that one of the keys to a successful private practice in architecture is that, whilst a good working relationship with several main contractors (who can be relied upon to keep their tenders at modest levels, take a pride in their craftmanship and abide by an agreed contract period) is of importance, what is of equal importance is a similar good working relationship with a wide range of small sub-contractors, craftsmen and suppliers, who each have their own particular specialist skills ranging from central heating installations, mosaic work and carpet laying to wood carving, mural painting and wrought ironwork, and many other skills and trades which contribute to the efficiency and character of a new building.

A one-man operation by an Anglesey wood-carver was one such sub-contractor who comes to mind. If something special in wood was required he was always able to perform, one of his best pieces for me being an over-life-sized, divided coffee pot carved in yew to form the door handles for a pair of armourplate glass doors at the entrance to a new coffee bar. His, most appropriate, surname was Selwood.

Edgar Fitton was another reliable sub-contractor for low-pressure, hot water, central heating systems. His business had been founded in pre-war years and Edgar was something of a relic from that period. When he first came to my office in Colwyn Bay he was immaculately dressed (below his bowler hat) in a black jacket and waistcoat, sporting his pocket-watch and chain, pin-striped trousers, a white shirt with a stiff winged collar and a grey silk tie. Although their head office was in Manchester, the Fittons lived in Colwyn Bay. In the 1950s many Manchester business people lived in North Wales and commuted to Manchester on the morning 'club' train, arriving in the city just before 10am and then leaving just after 4pm, to arrive back in Colwyn Bay at 6pm; just in time for the opening of the bar at the Colwyn Bay Club, conveniently situated just a hundred yards or so away from the railway station!

Pwllheli promenade as designed

Watkin Jones & Son of Bangor are one of the oldest building contracting firms in the British Isles, having been founded by the first Watkin in the late 18th century and having pursued their trade as undertakers and building contractors to the good people of Bangor through great-great-grandfather, great-grandfather, grandfather, father and then the incumbent Watkin in the 1950s. The Federation of Building Trade Employers keep a sort of league table of the date of foundation of their member firms and Watkin Jones & Sons are about eighth on the list nationally. First on the list is Durtnells of Kent whom I have used as a contractor in the London area. They claim a continuity of Durtnells in the firm since the 16th century, but this is built largely upon the fact that there is a Durtnell in the parish register of that time, in the village where they still have their headquarters, who is named as the master-carpenter of the village. One wonders however, whether there may have been one or two small gaps in the line of Durtnell business continuity over the last 500 years.

But back to Watkin Jones & Son. We had worked on many contracts for private houses and other buildings together and, one day, the then current Watkin asked me to go with him to Pwllheli on the Lleyn Peninsular where he had acquired several hundred yards of the, as yet, undeveloped promenade. How would I suggest that we should use the land for residential/holiday home purposes?

The promenade of Pwllheli stood well away from the town, separated from it in those days by a causeway across a large expanse of tidal flood plain. The dwellings were going to be overwhelmed by the bleakness of the situation and something was going to be needed to give the project distinctiveness. My solution was an almost continuous line of stepped terraced houses, each with first floor balconies looking south out to sea, the stepping and projections of the elevations giving each house individuality one from another, the terraces also being interspersed by a public house/restaurant and a shop.

Within these long terraces however, I also introduced the 'lighthouse', an eight storey structure of one/two-bedroomed apartments towering over the promenade and visible for miles around. Blackpool promenade enjoys a similar, rather taller, vertical feature!

The county planning officer, normally quite venturesome, was startled and was reluctant to give approval for the tower. He recommended to his committee that the application be referred to the Royal Fine Arts Commission for their observations with the rider that the committee were minded to refuse the application. I feared the worst but, surprisingly, the RFAC came out wholeheartedly for the scheme and the planning authority was left with no option but to approve the proposals.

My difficulties were still not yet over, as a dispute then occurred over the interpretation of the RIBA fee scale which had to go to arbitration for settlement. Fortunately again, my charges were wholly endorsed by the arbitrator and the Watkins paid up in full. We remained good friends thereafter and carried out many further projects together until the next generation Watkin took over (number 6!) when the nature of this time-honoured, local contracting business underwent fundamental change.

The sketches are for two of the stepped, terraced houses which were submitted for detailed planning approval. As I have grumbled earlier in the book, housing groups for speculative builders are not always built exactly to the approved designs and this proved to be the case in this instance. The photograph shows how the all-important stepped break between houses in the terraces was abandoned in favour of the bland, rather boring continuous facade, whilst retaining some elements of the individual house designs.

Houses as built

Stott house

Towards the end of the 1950s in my work as a private architect and as an Associate of the Royal Institute of British Architects, I discovered that the road to the more exalted title of Fellow of the Royal Institute of British Architects might be open for me.

The requirements were firstly that one must have attained the age of 30 (which I had just reached) and secondly that one must have supported oneself in private practice for more than seven years (which milestone was passed in 1957). Finally, one must have been responsible personally for the design, detailing and construction of a number of significant new buildings which would be assessed by a panel of eminent Fellows of the Institute appointed by the President. I totted up the number of projects for new buildings completed and was a little surprised to find that these had risen to well over 70 in the seven years since 1950 and I thought that at least one or two of those might aspire to the 'significant' description.

The full list of completed new buildings, with supporting drawings and photographs of the most respectable efforts were bundled off to the RIBA together with proposing and seconding signatures on the accompanying form. I was then delighted to be informed a few weeks later that I had been duly elected as a Fellow of the Royal Institute.

Little did I appreciate at that time that this event marked the beginning of the end of the 'special houses for special people' phase of my private practice which I had so much enjoyed in these early years. Larger, public projects were looming and, against that background, it became increasingly more difficult to take on commissions for individual houses and be assured of being able to devote the necessary personal time to seeing through a private house contract from start to finish. Assistants can be of immense value on large projects but can rarely be relied upon to sustain the devotion needed to ensure that the integrity of an original private house concept is retained entirely in the final bricks and mortar. One-off houses are ideally the realm of the one-man practice - or at least one man with no more than two or three assistants with whom he can maintain constant daily contact.

There were however, still many 'special houses for special people' to come, some of them, through their situation and the requirements of the client, holding much scope for interesting design solutions. One such house was for the Stott family in Trearddur Bay.

Albert Stott was a prominent Manchester business man, heading a close and active family. As the children grew out of school age they would gather together with Mr and Mrs Stott, as they had done from their earliest days, on three main occasions each year. Christmas was the obvious one, but there was always the family chalet skiing holiday in the early Spring and then the sailing holiday in Trearddur Bay in August.

From the shore at low tide

From the lane

Albert Stott became the Commodore of the Trearddur Bay Sailing Club and decided that this meant that he should endeavour to get a little closer to the water than their current Trearddur Bay holiday home, which stood all of 50 yards away from the beach! The old lifeboat house lying between the shore road to Ravenspoint and the sandy beach stood on the edge of about half an acre of undeveloped open ground linking the beach with the road. This had been eyed for many years by visitors to Trearddur Bay as the ideal site for a holiday house, but the Stotts managed to find the key to the purchase of the land.

The accommodation required to house the family was quite extensive but there was adequate land available to sprawl the largely single-storey house across the beach frontage. There was however, a stipulation for one room to be at first floor level to ensure that sailing races in the bay could be observed from start to finish. Another minor stipulation was the provision of an internal wind gauge powered from rotating cups and vane on the top of the chimney, with the gauge reading in a prominent place on the ground floor for all to judge the strength and direction of the wind throughout the day.

The Stotts have enjoyed their beach house for many years, gathering there each August for the Trearddur Bay sailing season. Quite coincidentally, one of their greatest friends, family to family, were the Davies family, our own immediate neighbours in Colwyn Bay, who also decamped to Trearddur Bay each August for the sailing. The eldest Davies boy, Peter, who rose to be the head of Reed International, Prudential and Sainsburys in quite rapid succession, to eventually become Sir Peter, was heard to recount, on his Desert Island Discs' stint, of his still enduring passion for a week or two's sailing each August in Trearddur Bay with his family - and, also, no doubt, with the Stotts.

*Nuclear homes - Kingsway
Housing*

In the late 1950s I was approached by the Kingsway Housing Association who had been asked to build an estate of what can only be described as 'middle-management' houses, to cater for staff of the Wylfa nuclear power station which was to be built in Anglesey. It was thought that 20 to 30 such houses would be required by the time of the commissioning of the new station. I was asked to assist in the location of a suitable site within easy access of the Wylfa site.

The new nuclear power station was, understandably, to be placed at what was probably the most remote place on the island along the shoreline. At the western extremities of Anglesey, it lay on open cliff-land, facing out across the Irish Sea to the distant Mountains of Mourne in Northern Ireland, some 80 miles away. Tree growth in this exposed area was almost absent and, particularly in the winter months, the environment tended to be bleak and inhospitable.

This approach from Kingsway took my mind back a few years to when we were befriended by the Carpenters, who lived close to the shoreline of north-west Anglesey in a similar position to the proposed nuclear power station. The house lay slightly behind the cliffs and, when we first visited them at home, Dorothy and I were surprised to find that, a few hundred yards up the drive to the house, we crested a hill to find ourselves driving around a large expanse of woodland nestling behind the hill and then seeing a fine Queen Anne style house across a small lake, well protected from the prevailing westerly winds from the sea by the hillside and woodland. The Carpenters were the surviving arm of what was probably the oldest of the landowning families in Anglesey, the full name of the family being Holland-Carpenter, with the Holland branch stemming from a still extant Elizabethan house, Plas Berw, in the village of Holland Arms in the centre of the island (see *Ancient Monuments in Anglesey* by the Royal Commission on Ancient and Historical Monuments in Wales). The couple had been uprooted from their lifetime home in Canada to take over the properties which Mr Carpenter had inherited from the previous life tenant of the estate. One of the most fascinating relics they had taken over when moving into their remote mansion was a white lace handkerchief encased in a glass-fronted box which was said to have been left by Queen Elizabeth I when she visited the family. It appeared to have been laundered before boxing.

I was later commissioned to deal with the re-slating of the leaking roof and to carry out other structural repairs to the fabric of the old house at Plas Berw, for which a government grant had been acquired. The family solicitors warned me that Plas Berw and the associated fields and marshlands of the upper end of the Cefni estuary had been occupied for some generations by a reclusive family, the present tenants being three, elderly, unmarried brothers of the family. They were known to be most hostile to visitors of any kind to their home and lands.

Sure enough, when I drove up to the farm gate with an assistant at the appointed time and date to conduct a survey of the roof, the gate was firmly closed and two of the brothers equipped with (presumably) loaded shotguns were straddling the ground on the farm side of the gate. I was required to substantiate my credentials before the gate would be opened, which, as the brothers were monoglot Welsh speakers, proved to be an uncomfortable process! We were however, eventually admitted to the house and I was surprised to find the interior in about the same form as might have been expected when the house was built in the 16th century. Bare-boarded oak flooring, oak panelled walls and shuttered, uncurtained windows, all furnished with oak benches and chairs, an oak refectory table, oak chests, four poster beds and little else.

A few months later, with essential renovations complete and roof leaks banished, good relations had been established with the brothers and visits to Plas Berw were rather more warmly welcomed. All this however, has little to do with the commission other than that it rapidly became clear that the nominee management for the new power station had little enthusiasm for housing arrangements which might be provided for them on the exposed cliffs of north-west Anglesey, with the shores of the Menai Straits on the other side of the island, some 20 miles away, being a preferred location.

A site for this group of houses was found at Llandegfan, on high ground above the Straits and, once again, enjoying the magnificent view of the Caernarfonshire mountains which are obtainable from eastern Anglesey. Some 20 houses were built for the Five Counties Housing Association in time for the opening of the power station. These nuclear power engineers were indisputedly special people and this Llandegfan estate was indeed built especially for these special people.

BATHING DIFFICULTIES

Sturla house

Reference has been made earlier to the plots of land at Ravenspoint which had been set aside for individually designed houses, tailored to the requirements of the purchasers of the plots. The nomination of myself as architect for several of these houses was stipulated by my perceptive client John Bibby, who believed that it was important to ensure that integrated designs for the houses and their surroundings preserved the character and value of the estate as a whole.

This did not necessarily make for easy commissions for the architect as the clients were not coming forward as the result of recommendations or because they had seen previous completed projects, but because they were obliged to do so. This resulted in some severe and time-consuming conflicts on aesthetic issues for one or two of these special houses.

The first house illustrated was for the Sturla family and was located on a large rock outcrop placed centrally in the estate. In an endeavour to prevent the house becoming something of a pimple in this prominent, exposed position, floor levels were adjusted to follow ground levels and a roof slope was adopted which echoed the slope of the rock upon which the house was founded, thus ensuring that the structure worked with the ground contours rather than against them as would have been the case with a more conventional roof. This was not one of the houses where complaints arose from the clients on the aesthetics of the design.

A house where such conflicts did arise occupied the site at the extreme corner of the estate on the cliff edge. The name given to the house by the Sucksmiths was Ponta Delgada as the site reminded them of a rocky promontory in the Azores where they had spent a holiday. In reaching a final design for the house it was necessary to override a number of inappropriate requests for the exterior treatment of the structure and the relationship with the client never really recovered from that contretemps. In discussions with staff in my absence, Mr Sucksmith always referred to me as 'tache' rather than by my name (I sported a modest moustache in those days, as now) and I recollect that an argument as to whether or not we had specified and installed a large enough bath to accommodate Mr Sucksmith's quite ample form went on for several years after the occupation of the house.

Sucksmith house

Another Ravenspoint client with whom I saw very much more eye to eye on aesthetic matters was Geoffrey McLean. He was a housebuilder from Wolverhampton, even then approaching national status, who went on to become one of the most successful housebuilding firms in the country, both financially and aesthetically. I recall being most impressed on a visit to his offices in Wolverhampton by the logical and efficient way in which his building land requirements and the disposition of future sites were charted in his office system. Mr McLean bought three of these sites and I designed and detailed individual houses for each site, but he did not go forward with the houses and the land lay fallow for several years before being sold on to others. One or two of these plots still remain undeveloped and the house which was built, without my guidance, is much out of character with the remainder of the estate.

Mr Howard worked in Manchester and he remains in my mind as the client at Ravenspoint who would telephone me in my Colwyn Bay office towards the end of fine mornings to say that he would like to meet on site immediately after lunch if I did not have any other engagements. The race then started to see whether I could drive the 40 miles from Colwyn Bay to Trearddur Bay in time to be there before Mr Howard, who was on his way to Manchester airport to fly his own private plane to RAF Valley where a taxi would be waiting to take him the few remaining miles to Ravenspoint. He usually won, if the usual summer crop of caravans was being shunted slowly along the old tortuous A55 through North Wales.

Dr Lloyd Lewis house

Dr Lloyd Lewis was a general medical practitioner who had a house and surgery right in the centre of Bangor, just below the cathedral and the High Street. The house stood in an acre of gardens and was a haven of tranquillity at the heart of the busy city centre.

The Caernarfonshire Planning Committee determined that Bangor was in need of a consolidated shopping centre to complement the mile long High Street which carried all the existing shops and businesses of the city, curling along the foot of a virtually impassable cliff which edged the open plateau lying above the urbanization (and which followed the line of the ancient high-water mark below the cliff). It was thus the case that the Lloyd Lewis garden represented about the only space which could be utilized for the new shopping area in the city centre and it was designated accordingly as such in the County Development Plan.

With detailed plans approved by the planning authority for the new shopping complex, there was little option for the Lloyd Lewis family but to up sticks and move elsewhere. They found a plot in a quiet residential area in Upper Bangor, unlikely to be invaded by supermarket barons, and lying close to the University. The land sloped steeply down below the road, but commanded views across the city to the cathedral, the harbour and the Straits beyond. I was invited over for luncheon one day at the soon-to-be-demolished house to meet this delightful family and to hear about their requirements for the new house.

The design solution was for a neighbourly, four-square rendered brickwork and slate-roofed house, embellished by a storey of squared rubble stonework on the approach side of the house. The house was built well below the public road but at a level which provided for a not too steep access for cars to the garage.

Apart from the contract period and the completion of the house in 1962, my strongest recollection of this contract was the call I received from a cross Dr Lloyd Lewis in 1962/63 winter to say that the mains water supply to the house had frozen and why had I not ensured that the incoming main had been laid deep enough to make certain that it could not freeze up. Up to 1963, convention was that, providing a watermain was laid not less than 1'6" (450 mm) below ground level it would lie below the level that persistent frost could reach in a British winter. The winter of 1962/63 however, experienced the deepest and longest period of frost that had been seen for very many years and that frost reached and stayed down well below the 1'6" below-ground-level of the main for several continuous weeks from January to March.

I had great sympathy for the Lloyd Lewis family in their predicament as, the previous summer, we had moved into a different house (built in 1925) and my family were experiencing precisely the same problems with the 50-yard long water main lying below the drive. My solution for the Lloyd Lewis house was exactly the same as I adopted for my own house - one of the newly marketed plastic water lines laid along the surface of the drive, temporarily connected to the mains in the public road instead of the frozen pipe and brought into the house at the same point as the frozen main. The plastic of the pipe protected the mains water quite well from the frost and it warmed up enough to melt any ice which did accumulate in the surface pipe overnight with the aid of the sun, or blower heaters if necessary.

It was several weeks before it was safe to dispense with the surface plastic pipes and to revert to the now frost-free buried pipes. Arrangements were however, made to lower the Lloyd Lewis incoming main by another six inches as a precaution against a repeat of the 1963 mini-ice age and I ensured that all future incoming residential water mains were laid at that lower level.

This, no doubt, was the sort of problem which Jerome K Jerome (the author of *Three Men in a Boat*) had in mind when he had one of the characters of his novel *They and I* (1909) observing:

> "I want a house that has got over all its troubles; I don't want to spend the rest of my life bringing up a young and inexperienced house."

Wands house

Mrs Wands owned a plot of land in Llandegfan, Anglesey, high above the nearby Menai Straits and sloping gently towards the south. She wondered whether it was large enough to take two single-storey houses, one for herself and one for a companion. My conclusion was that it would be difficult to accommodate two such detached houses on the site satisfactorily but, with care, the site could accommodate two semi-detached, dormer-roofed, one-and-a-half-storey houses. Instructions were taken to proceed with the design, detail and construction of these two houses.

There was nothing particularly notable about these houses. The roofs of the houses were aligned to follow differing building lines without any visually disturbing break in the shared roof slopes. The two houses, with slight variations in elevational treatment thus blended into the sloping ground in what can be described as an appropriate degree of anonymity.

This quality of relative anonymity in architecture is not one which receives much attention in the architectural press. There are many occasions when an architect must, or should, strive for that quality in particular positions or circumstances. Perhaps the most obvious example of the need for anonymity is seen when designing for new buildings in an historic neighbourhood such as a conservation area. Slavishly copying the style and detail of the adjoining historic structures will seldom provide the right answers in these circumstances; indeed such an approach, using shiny new mechanically correct materials can often give an incongruous appearance to the new structure, creating a parody of, and thus detracting from, the quality of the surrounding historic buildings. The answer is preferably a modest, relatively plain, simple structure utilizing materials compatible with the local vernacular, but fading into the background in relation to the much older neighbours.

I recall being faced with a problem of this nature on a large scale, a few years later than the Wands' house, when I was commissioned to design an extension to one of the very first planned small towns in Wales at Tremadoc in Caernarfonshire. Tremadoc had been built by William Madocks in the earliest years of the 19th century when he was the Member of Parliament for Boston in Lincolnshire. With the assistance of John Williams, his local agent, he built firstly a two-mile long barrage to enclose a thousand acres of tidal flood plain forming part of the Glaslyn estuary within which to build the new town of Tremadoc. He then built Tremadoc to a T-shaped plan with the town hall on the axis of the T, hard against the rocky hillside at the edge of the former tidal plain. Madocks travelled frequently by stagecoach over the 200 miles from London, supervising the construction of the little town and organising the race meetings and theatre performances which were features of the early years of the venture. He earned the nickname of Th'Improver for these extraordinary achievements.

Tremadoc had retained its compact planned identity for 150 years at the time I was commissioned to extend the little town, which covered an area of only five acres or so of the reclaimed flood plain. The extension to Tremadoc proposed by the local authority was to double the size of the historic settlement. I was heard to observe when first contemplating the design work for the 60 dwellings, that the only way of making certain that the integrity of the existing town was preserved was to put all the new houses underground! In the event however, the completed extension to Tremadoc was quite well-received and was given a Highly Commended status by the RIBA/Welsh Office Housing Medal assessors. The article in the *Architect's Journal* at the time ventured the title 'Th'Improver Improved?' to their feature on the estate.

Old Tremadoc

New Tremadoc

Tremadoc is a long way from the Wands' house in size and scope, but the two case histories had similarities on this need for a degree of anonymity in design. It was thus a little surprising when the Wands' houses were given an award by the Civic Trust, thus demonstrating that there were others who appreciated that studied anonymity in architecture was entirely appropriate in certain circumstances.

COTTAGES IN THE PARK

Tan-y-Bwlch cottages - Bibby

The name of John Bibby, of Ravenspoint ilk, crops up yet again in this example of holiday-cottage building in North Wales. Plas Tan-y-Bwlch was an enormous stone mansion built on a hillside above Maentwrog on the Mawddch Estuary in Merioneth and surrounded by several score acres of parkland. The estate came onto the market in the early 1960s, complete with the parkland and several cottages and bothies in the grounds. It was bought outright by John Bibby and the first I knew about the purchase was a call asking me to meet him at the Plas later in the week.

Mr Bibby had bought the property with only the vaguest ideas about what might be done with it. Certainly the cottages and other small buildings would make attractive holiday cottages and the first task was to obtain the necessary permissions and to carry out the conversion and refurbishment of these small buildings. He had a working foreman in his employment who looked after the fabric of his properties and who brought in a team of independent tradesmen, as required, to carry out the work. Members of this team were brought to Plas Tan-y-Bwlch to undertake the work on the cottage conversions as the detailed proposals were approved by the local authorities, camping out in the mansion for the period of their work.

What to do with the mansion was another matter. The floor area extended to many thousands of square feet and the fabric was showing signs of distress. There were ideas of a conference or holiday centre, but the costs of conversion and repair to effect those uses were daunting. More support for these concepts would be needed before any such scheme could be implemented. I had always yearned for the chance to create a new holiday village within an idyllic setting and this parkland area stretching up the hillside from the water's edge, and dominated by the massive presence of the stone-built Plas might provide just that opportunity. The difficulty facing the holiday-village concept was that tourist enterprises of this sort were not at all popular with the Welsh local authorities, particularly in such environmentally sensitive areas as this. Fortunately, to the west of the mansion, there was an expanse of light woodland in which a number of cottages could be located without significant disturbance to the tree cover. I suggested that, rather than seeking an outline planning permission for the proposals, which was almost certain to be refused as a matter of principle, we should go straight to a tree survey and full details of the proposals so that the planners could see exactly what was intended.

Survey and design drawings accordingly were prepared for the location of some 20 new cottages within the grounds of the mansion and fully detailed drawings of the cottage types were submitted. A controversial feature of these designs was that a low, single-pitched roof was proposed for these small dwellings rather than the almost obligatory steep-pitched slated roofs of the district which would have made these modest proposals entirely uneconomic. As the cottages were to be contained within the grounds of the mansion and set well away from any other buildings, I felt that a good case could be argued for not using traditional slate roofs in this position.

In the event, approval of the proposals by the planning committee went through quite smoothly. Construction of the first group of cottages commenced almost at once using the working foreman/imported craftsmen, in-house system of the Bibby set-up. Using this system, it was necessary for me to give rather more than the usual degree of supervision to the work in order to ensure that the detailing was properly honoured, but the first few dwellings were completed in time for the opening of the next holiday season. As part of the commission, I implemented proposals for the furnishing and equipping of the cottages so that they were ready to receive visitors without further input at the beginning of the season.

The mansion from the cottages

The intention was to complete a further group of cottages each winter in time for the next season opening but, before the beginning of the next season, John Bibby received an approach from the County Council who had, rather belatedly, appreciated the potential for the mansion and grounds for founding a conference centre and the sale went through before the next group of cottages was commenced. The first group of cottages had however, been entered for the current Civic Trust Award assessment for the county and I was delighted to receive a yet further Civic Trust Award for this small group of holiday cottages.

Lomax house

This house was designed and built for Mr Lomax. The site lies below Llys Helig Drive in Llandudno, a lane branching off the private road which encircles the Great Orme headland for the four miles or so between West Shore and the Llandudno pier. At the time the house was built, it marked the western extremity of residential development along Llys Helig Drive, although since the 1960s several more houses have been built to finish off the extent of the permitted development along this southern flank of the Orme. The Lomax house was built a few hundred yards further along the cliff from the Twist house which is the subject of an earlier vignette.

The height of the cliff forming this flank of the Great Orme rises as one advances towards the west and there was a drop of about 30 feet to the beach from the building plateau which lay below the roadway and up to the edge of the cliff. The site, although enjoying magnificent views across the mouth of the Conwy estuary to the mountains beyond and then round to the coast of Anglesey in the west, was in a most exposed position in the teeth of the frequent high winds off the sea from that direction. The house was therefore designed as a long low structure, squatting low on the cliff, but also enjoying the protection of the mass of the Great Orme from cold winds from the north, whilst receiving sunshine from early morning until late evening from the open aspect to the south.

The difficulty with this site, and with most of the other similar house sites ranged along the south-facing cliff at the foot of the Great Orme was that the scree forming the cliff was gradually eroding away with the action of the sea, wind and rain on the bottom of the cliff. Every three or four years a further metre or two of cliff would cascade into the sea so that, given the same rate of erosion, many of the Llys Helig Drive houses would be at risk in a hundred years or so.

The issue which has become more evident since the 1960s is that of global warming. If we were to believe the environmentalists (and the politicians!) rising sea levels will accelerate the pace of erosion much more quickly to the extent that the Lomax house, and many of the other adjacent properties, could be at risk in a much shorter period than a hundred years. The Great Orme promontory has however, been in place for many millions of years and, in that time, it has seen ice ages and sub-tropical periods come and go over periods extending for hundreds of thousands of years, with changes of one or two degrees in ambient temperatures often occuring several times within a century. It is therefore difficult to accept that the interpretation of current minor movements of temperature as artificially induced global warming are anything other than politically motivated scaremongering. The statistician Bjorn Lomberg in his 250,000 word, 200 graph treatise on this subject (*The Skeptical Environmentalist*, published in 2001 by the Cambridge Press), page by page, table by table and graph by graph meticulously and methodically demolishes the case for many such environmental myths (including the likely effect and extent of global warming) in a most eloquent manner. More recently Professor Emeritus Philip Stott of the University of London in an article in *The Times* has summarised exactly the same case. The residents of Llys Helig Drive can rest secure in their beds in the knowledge that their houses are safe for many generations to come.

Great Orme backdrop

As a postscript to the Lomax house, I did design a house for myself and my family to be built at the very western extremity of the permitted development, a point which was marked by a coastal gun position in the 1939/45 war and which gave the name of 'Gunsite' to the proposed house. Because of the exposed position, the house was designed to surround an enclosed atrium to be used as outdoor living in windy weather. Our summer enthusiasm for proceeding with the house ebbed away however, when the site was re-visited in a late autumn gale when we found it difficult to stand up in what would have been the position of the front door of the house. The project was quietly shelved.

THE FOUNDATION OF CHAMPAGNE

Glazebrook house

The Glazebrooks had their business in Liverpool and lived nearby on the Wirral. They were a young couple with very young children and were anxious to move out into the country, but to still remain within commuting distance of Liverpool for three or four days each week. They were therefore not able to penetrate too far into North Wales for their new home, but had family connections in the Denbigh area, which was just about on the boundary of a reasonable commuting distance.

The site for their new house comprised several acres of parkland forming the grounds of a large house which had been demolished in the immediate postwar years, but the drive and grounds, although rather overgrown, provided a fine setting for a new house. The house was isolated from other dwellings and was well outside any designated development area. Planning permission was however, given because of the residential history of the site.

Large dwellings in extensive grounds became increasingly difficult to maintain in the depression years of the 1930s and, towards the end of that decade it was possible to acquire a five or six-bedroomed house in an acre or so of grounds for little more than £500 in many parts of the country - representing about one year's salary for the middle-classes in those days. Many such houses became unoccupied towards the end of the decade and remained so during the war years, unless they were requisitioned for war purposes.

With income tax levels rising to above 87.5% of a person's income in the immediate postwar years and with domestic staff at a premium, these fine houses remained empty and decaying. In many cases demolition was the only answer for these structures and there were thus numbers of such sites available when it became possible to build largish new houses once again in the 1960s.

This house was designed and built for the Glazebrooks on the site of the original house, making good use of the surrounding terraced areas retained from the former mansion, which areas were marked out by the carved stone balustrading of those original terraces.

The entrance front

When work commenced on site on the Glazebrook house, the first discovery was that the grassed and apparently flat site for the house concealed a range of cellars which had simply been filled with rubble from the demolished house, all of which had to be excavated out and concreted over before building work could start on the superstructure. During that preliminary clearance work a minor frisson of excitement occurred when a cache of unopened champagne bottles was discovered amongst the rubble in the cellars. I was told over the telephone by the foreman that a bottle had been opened and that it had been found to be undrinkable, but I did not have the opportunity of testing that finding for myself and it was rather strange that every one of the 'undrinkable' bottles had disappeared from the site by the time of my next visit two days later!

Wilde flats - Menaifron

The Wilde name has appeared in an earlier vignette and a reference was made there to other property holdings in Anglesey. The land and buildings lay in the extreme southern corner of the island, close to the shoreline of the Menai Straits and opposite Caernarfon on the mainland shore. There is evidence that the site at Menaifron had been the Roman landing point in Anglesey from their fort at Segontium which lay above the present Caernarfon town centre.

The large house at Menaifron which had been central to these holdings had been demolished in the immediate postwar years, leaving the farmhouses and the cottages of the estate intact. I had carried out alterations and improvements to the largest of the farmhouses at an earlier date for the Wilde daughter and son-in-law who were responsible for the management of the estate. Also left intact was the stable block for the old mansion which lay between the site of the house and the shore.

My instructions from the Wildes were to devise proposals for the conversion and renovation of the stable block to provide a flat for a housekeeper on the ground floor and a self-contained flat for themselves on the first floor for weekend and holiday visits. The accommodation which could be provided within the shell of the existing building, without extension, was a small sitting room, bedroom/bathroom and a large kitchen on the ground floor and a large drawing room, bedroom/bathroom and kitchenette on the first floor. The windows at first floor level, facing south-east, took as much advantage as possible of the fine views across the widening Straits to Caernarfon, the passage dominated by the 14th century castle and against the backcloth of the mountains of Snowdonia.

This conversion of an existing stone-built stable block to domestic accommodation resulted in the receipt of a 13th Civic Trust Award or Commendation for the practice. Of these 13 awards, six had been for individual or small groups of private dwellings (all of which are illustrated here), the other seven awards received up to the end of the 1960s being for commercial, charity or local authority projects.

By the time of the Menaifron conversion I was well familiar with the problems inherent in the conversion and renovation of the traditional buildings of Wales. In this book, some 70 to 80 individual dwellings are reviewed or mentioned, most of which were completely new structures, with only ten per cent or so being major conversions and virtual reconstructions of existing buildings. These 70/80 dwellings however, represent less than ten per cent of the total number of commissions received up to the date of this project, the job number for Menaifron being 651. A great many of the more than 500 commissions which do not feature here were for minor extensions or alterations to existing dwellings, including Improvement Grant projects which called for a dry, warm and well-ventilated dwelling in a good state of repair on the conclusion of the work, as a condition of the grant for the installation of modern services.

The main problems encountered with these old buildings were the solid stone walls which, towards the end of the winter would see the wind-blown rains penetrating past the drenched outer sections of the stone walling, to reach the inside plasterwork, particularly around window and door jambs, a lack of overhang at eaves and verges resulting in the penetration of rainwater into the upper parts of external walls; broken, missing and disintegrating roof slates and nails; dry rot in roof and flooring timbers; rising damp in the walling from ground moisture and many other similar problems, all requiring consideration and attention before one could begin to consider the internal and external changes and improvements to the property. The Menaifron stable buildings were no exception to this roll-call of structural problems.

The buildings in their setting

Imeson house

Mr Imeson was a solicitor who worked from home in Menai Bridge without the aid of supporting staff. I was commissioned by him and Mrs Imeson to carry out alterations to their house, which were duly completed.

The next I heard from the Imesons was a year or two later when I was telephoned to say that they proposed to move house and workbase to Penhryn Bay and that they had acquired a plot of land on the western side of the Rhos-on-Sea golf-course which enjoyed a frontage, and gate access, to the golf-course. They wished to build a house on the plot and asked me to act as their architect for the project.

The house illustrated here was built to occupy the full width of the fairly restricted frontage, but leaving a reasonable rear garden area between the house and the boundary with the golf-course. One of the more unusual hazards experienced during the building contract was the vulnerability of the workmen to the occasional sliced drive from a nearby tee which would come whistling over the boundary fence, landing with the force of small arms fire on the emerging structure - and the workmen. An emergency extension of the original scope of the contract was consequently ordered as a variation, taking the form of a high mesh fence on that portion of the boundary in the direct line of fire from the offending tee.

Mr Imeson represented an old, but dying, tradition of the family solicitor with a modest client list who was able to keep all professional activities in his own hands and without a presence in the High Street. These one-man solicitor operations were most useful for fellow professionals, not least because the normal cost of a consultation and one or two letters to a client urging an overdue fee account would rarely exceed a guinea or so.

With the vast, real increases which have occurred in solicitors' charges in recent years, it would be difficult to find a solicitor who would now carry out that service for less than £50 and, given the slightest complication in the service, a charge of over £100. This enormous escalation in solicitors' (and counsels') fees has been far greater than has been the case with other professions (particularly architects!) and it has become increasingly difficult for the private individual or small businessman to even consult a solicitor, let alone to contemplate going to law to pursue a business problem.

In these early days of practice in the 1950s and early 1960s, there were only two occasions when it was necessary for me to go to the High Court to recover fees. The first of these was when, after agreeing a scale of charges with a building contractor for obtaining detailed planning permissions for an estate of 40 houses of varying types and then obtaining those permissions, less than half of the fees were paid and payment of the remainder was refused on the basis of an *Alice in Wonderland* interpretation of the agreed fee scale.

I exercised patience, hoping that wiser counsels would prevail, but was then astounded to see houses being built on the land which, whilst bearing an unmistakeable resemblance to the approved designs, differed in detail from my drawings. On further investigation I discovered that my drawings had been traced over, with minor variations, by the builder's own draughtsman (no doubt with the avoidance of fees in view) and had been submitted for revised planning permissions. What was simply a fee dispute thus developed into a copyright claim which ran on for a further year or two. The managing director of the firm then died suddenly and his co-directors were astounded to learn of the running dispute which had occurred. They paid all the outstanding fees in full, plus the costs to date on the action, without further delay.

The house illustrated here from another site, designed for the same builder is fairly typical of the small seaside cottages designed for the disputed site although not, of course, being the unbuilt designs which were the subject of the dispute.

The second occasion concerned a caravan site mogul who owned beach frontage sites for several hundred caravans in North Wales and who wished to extend his empire. He told me that he had negotiated a £250,000 facility from his bank, secured on his caravan sites, and that he proposed to use that facility to obtain new sites and new permissions. He referred to sites on which he held options in Malta, the Isle of Man and elsewhere in North Wales. My reaction (not being a caravan site enthusiast) was that, whilst I would be happy to pursue planning applications to develop the sites as holiday villages with permanent chalet-type accommodation, I would be unable to get involved with caravan site proposals. It was agreed that we would go forward with the sites on that basis. My new client had also just purchased a house in the area and required extensive alterations and extensions to be carried out to the house.

We visited the Isle of Man together the following week to inspect his attractive coastal valley site and I was pleased to receive confirmation from the planning officer that caravan sites would be unacceptable to the Island Government. His new house and the potential holiday village sites in North Wales were also inspected. I then put separate teams to work on the three projects simultaneously. Whilst that work was proceeding, yet further sites were brought forward for my consideration and sketch proposals. After a few months' work I had obtained a detailed planning permission from the Isle of Man Government for a holiday village of some 40 linked chalets and for a similar number of holiday flats on a North Wales site. Work was under way on the building contract for the new house extensions and alterations. The site in Malta awaited an inspection visit.

Interim fee accounts had been submitted on account of the work in progress but no fees had been received a month or two after submission of the fee accounts. Fees were promised but not received and, whilst the work was still proceeding solicitors were consulted on the matter and (one guinea!) letters were written. When fees were still not received, I ceased work on all projects and writs were issued.

Defences and counter-claims were received, most surprisingly partly based on the contention that our client had wanted permissions for new caravan sites and what he had received were planning permissions for permanent holiday villages, albeit some of which were already under construction. The case proceeded to the High Court and was heard by the Official Referee. After a three-day hearing, judgment was handed down entirely in my favour in respect of the overall £4,250 claimed in fees (£75,000 in present day prices) plus all costs. Truly a nail-biting few days.

One becomes less trusting of new clients (particularly owners of caravan sites requiring urgent extensive work on numerous projects) after experiences such as this.

56

HOUSING LIST DWELLINGS

Semi-detached houses

The Council of the Royal Borough of Caernarfon became my clients in 1960 for various public housing projects which do not qualify for inclusion in this book of special individual houses for special people. After the programme of local authority housebuilding initiated by the Conservatives and continued by the incoming Labour Government in 1964 there was a reaction back to a realization that it was the private house market which required a stimulus. That period is a little later than the period covered by this book, but this example of private housebuilding was a recognition by the Royal Borough of Caernarfon that there could be too many council houses in a town. My instructions for the development of this site close to the outskirts of the town therefore were to design proposals for a group of 30 or so detached and semi-detached houses which would be suitable for selling, rather than letting, to families on the Council's waiting list for houses to let and on which the Council would be able to make 100% mortgage advances.

Proposals were prepared for the site and tenders were invited for the construction of the complete estate and associated landscape works. A brochure illustrating the houses and the prices required to cover the cost of the land, construction costs and professional fees in respect of each house (ensuring that all the Council's costs would be recovered from the sales) was designed and printed. Construction work commenced, but every house on this small estate was sold before even one house was completed, including one of the several one-off houses on the prime sites to the Borough Surveyor. All work on the houses was completed within a 12-month period and 30 families (special people), previously all living in rented accommodation, became home-owners at the instigation of the local Council. All in all, a most successful initiative by this forward-looking Council. Two of the standard house-types on this estate are illustrated here.

Detached house type

Following the completion of this estate, I was attending a ward meeting of my local political party when requests were made for proposals for motions which might be submitted to the Constituency Committee for consideration ahead of the pending annual Party Conference. It seemed to me that, given the importance of the national house building programme, this way of using the expertise of local authorities to bolster the ownership of private houses was something that might have some political appeal and I ventured the suggestion.

The next I heard of the matter was a request to prepare a short paper to appear before a Constituency General Meeting and to address the meeting on the subject in company with one or two other individuals who had also been selected to put forward proposals for the Constituency motion for the Party Conference. My address seemed to be quite well received but I did not expect to be further involved. Out of the blue however, a week or two later, I received a return rail ticket to the seaside Conference venue together with a confirmation of an hotel reservation for me for the period of the Conference and a note to say that I would be putting the motion to Conference for endorsement at a particular time and date.

The cold sweats which resulted from the realization that a spontaneous suggestion made at a local ward committee meeting was propelling me onto the platform of a national party conference lasted for some weeks until, with considerable relief, I heard the announcement that all party conferences were to be cancelled because of a General Election which had been called for that October. Moral - never volunteer specialist knowledge to lay committees unless one can be quite sure where such initiatives might lead.

57

RED AND ROAD RIBBONS

Gordon Roberts house

There were two firms of solicitors in Llangefni in the 1950s. The larger of the two main firms remains in memory largely because of the massive green cast iron letterpress (circa 1880) which stood on a table in the outer office. Many outgoing and incoming letters were still written in longhand and the letterpress was used to imprint copies of these penned letters for the files and court bundles. The 'technology' of this time-honoured, pre-Xerox system still escapes me.

The second, smaller firm was a two-solicitor practice headed by Mr Gordon Roberts, a small, wiry, elderly gentleman who was renowned locally for effectiveness on his feet in court work. He was nearing, or was perhaps already past, normal retirement age but remained very active and fully in charge of his office - and his clients. Over the years there had been an immense accumulation of rather vaguely filed documentation, tied up with red ribbon, which overflowed out of cupboards and onto tables and floors through the suite of offices, much of it seemingly having gathered the dust of decades where it lay.

His partner was Sylvia Gordon Roberts, his daughter, whose constant endeavour was to bring some semblance of order into the office records but who was forbidden to touch any of the older files as her father knew exactly where everything was and relied entirely on his memory to find a particular document when needed. Mr Gordon Roberts retired eventually, at least partly, and his daughter was handed full charge of the practice. Virtually her first action was to ask me to draw up proposals for a re-modelling of their office building, providing modern amenities, a new efficient filing room, an attractive reception area, the removal of dust and redecoration throughout. The result was a fine new suite of offices - although some clients still retained a lingering nostalgia for the old Dickensian atmosphere which had been banished.

A few years later, Miss Gordon Roberts decided to have a new house built and she asked me to undertake this further commission. The site chosen was on the eastern outskirts of town, amongst other relatively new houses fronting the old Menai Bridge/Holyhead coach road. The plot was owned by a local landowner, a client of my practice called Roger Lloyd for whom I had prepared recently an extended layout to the rear of the group of houses in question for planning permission purposes.

Apart from his landholdings on the outskirts of Llangefni, Roger Lloyd owned coastal land on the edge of the fishing village of Moelfre, other land around his home in the centre of the island three or four miles out of Llangefni and further landholdings in South Caernarfonshire. I had also prepared proposals and obtained planning permission for some of the Moelfre land and had undertaken work in connection with the Caernarfonshire land and buildings.

Roger Lloyd did not farm any of the landholdings himself, being a land agent by profession, but had tenant farmers spread across the two counties. All of this, rather incredibly, was run from a small estate office in the cobbled stable courtyard of his home - a former tackroom. His sole assistance was provided by a young man called Huw, learning the profession of a land agent, whose first job on arrival each morning in winter was to light the tackroom fire and trim the oil lamp for use later in the day, electricity not yet having reached the rural centre of the island.

I was always most happy to be invited to the estate office for afternoon consultations as tea time at Tre-Ysgawen, to which I was usually invited, was a serious matter. The dining room table would be laid with a white lace cloth, the table groaning with plates of white and brown bread and butter, homemade jams and with a freshly baked sponge cake occupying a central position on the table, all graciously presided over by Mrs Roger Lloyd in front of a crackling log fire. Occasions to be savoured for many years hence and well recollected now over 40 years on.

The house for Miss Gordon Roberts illustrated here was designed and built as part of a line of one-off houses facing on to an ancient highway in what used to be termed 'ribbon development', a form of layout which has been frowned upon by planning authorities since the 1940s. Given generous sized plots, good quality houses and a lightly trafficked public highway however, limited groups of such houses on the outskirts of a town can add much to the character of a settlement and they have the virtue that the attractive fronts of the houses face the public road and not the backs as so often occurs nowadays in new highway-engineer-inspired estate road layouts.

*Llys Dulas estate cottage
renovation*

The Tattons had silk and nylon factories in Staffordshire. Following a rather serious car accident, Mr Tatton decided to spend more time away from his business affairs and he bought a large estate on the north coast of Anglesey. Central to the estate was a large mansion, Llys Dulas, which had a 17th century core, but with extensive additions through the centuries to Victorian times. The mansion was however, in a poor state of repair and had been used by the tenants of the previous owners as an indoor chicken farm. The parkland surrounding the mansion extended to some 250 acres, including frontages to the sheltered beaches of Dulas Bay and also to the open Irish Sea coastline.

The history of my work with the Tattons extends back to the early days of the practice, although this vignette is centred around a house which was built at the end of the 'special houses for special people' period which is the subject of this book. The estate included numerous cottages, and farmhouses on land outside the home park and the first commission received in 1955 was to make one of the vacant houses habitable for Mr and Mrs Tatton for their personal use whilst they were in Anglesey and whilst they were contemplating the future of the estate. This first conversion and renovation is illustrated here.

There then followed further commissions for such renovations of existing cottages and these properties were furnished and let as holiday cottages as they were all situated close to the fine beaches of northern Anglesey.

The bathing chalet as renovated

At the end of a long tree-lined grassy avenue running east away from the mansion, there was a tortuous footpath and steps leading down the cliff face to a fine sandy, semi-private beach and, on a ledge close to the foot of the cliff, there was a stone-built bathing house, built in the mid-19th century and used for beach-side picnics and family bathing parties from the big house. The chalet overlooks the golden sand of the beach and, out at sea beyond the beach lies a small island near enough to the house to be able to observe the resident seal colony at work and play along the shore of the island. Mr Tatton decided that this idyllic position was a more amenable one for their summertime stays at Llys Dulas and I was commissioned to make the little structure habitable for short stays.

One of the difficulties was that there was little space available alongside the chalet for extensions and, at the rear of the building, there was an eight foot high stone retaining wall holding back the rather crumbly cliff, only three feet or so from the back wall of Portabello - as the beach house was called.

About a year after the completion of this contract, during the winter months, I received a call to say that a crisis had arisen at the cottage. On reaching the site, I found that the one hundred-year old stone retaining wall had bulged and collapsed after several days of heavy and continuous rains. The collapsed wall was itself now being retained only by the rear wall of the cottage for a length of several feet and any further movement could well have resulted in Portabello cottage ending up on the beach below.

Our structural engineers were called in and a programme of re-building and strengthening the retaining wall was devised with them. The work was put in hand as a matter of extreme urgency and the retaining wall retained once again.

Portabello from the beach

Attention turned next to the mansion itself. Despite the chickens, the 17th century core of the mansion was in good shape; built almost entirely in oak from the estate, it seemed good for several more centuries, which was far from being the case with the later extensions which had completely overwhelmed the original house and had made it difficult to identify where that structure was within the complexity of the later additions. A detailed survey of the buildings made it possible to see that the original house was an attractive surviving whole and was of a size and scale which, with careful restoration and the provision of modern services, could make a fine and comfortable home, entirely suitable to become the centrepiece of the estate once again. Recommendations were therefore drawn up for the demolition of about four-fifths of the existing mansion and the restoration of the historic core. The costs of the exercise were however, most formidable and the Tattons set aside the proposals for a while to consider other alternatives.

The main problem with the beach house site was that vehicular traffic could approach only within about a hundred yards of the cottage and the pedestrian access down from that point was steep and tortuous. The cliff face, as we had learned only too well, was too friable and unstable to support a simple extension of the avenue. The consulting engineer, Tony Baines, whom we had brought in to advise on the retaining wall problem, was able to devise proposals which would allow us, at some expense, to support a hairpin continuation of the driveway across the friable ground right down to the edge of the cliff where the drive was to be terminated. As the proposals developed it was decided that a short, further structurally complex extension of the drive would permit the construction of a garage at the highest level of the chalet 'extensions' which were then at the design stage.

Given that vehicular access to a high level garage, I was able to design proposals for a new house which, on several levels, linked the new garage accommodation with the beach cottage at the lower level, protected by substantial reinforced concrete retaining walls built against the cliff face. The resulting complex can be seen in the photograph taken from the beach below.

This new house does not follow the traditional Anglesey domestic vernacular, although it does employ the white rendered walls which go so well with such beachside sites. The layered sections of the house linking the lower and upper floor levels did not lend themselves to a more traditional approach and, as the site was a completely isolated one within a private park, it did seem appropriate to adopt a free-form approach to the structure. A possible criticism of the completed house might well be that it exhibited a little too much influence from exotic new Spanish coastal houses which had been observed by the architect during the course of a Majorcan holiday taken during the design stages!

Hanson beach cottage

The Hansons were friends of the Tattons from Staffordshire. On the Llys Dulas estate and just beyond the home park, there was a small cottage lying slightly above high-water mark on the shore of Dulas Bay. The Hansons acquired the cottage from the estate and asked me to prepare proposals for alterations and renovations to the rather dilapidated structure and to extend the accommodation to twice the original size.

To achieve adequate headroom in the living areas without changing the proportions of the existing façades it was necessary to lower the ground floor by a foot. Because external walls of traditional cottages in Anglesey did not have foundations, but were simply built up from large stones laid just below ground level, it was necessary to underpin the walls before constructing the new, lower floor slab. The roof was re-slated with overhangs to barge boards and eaves and the inside faces of external walls were lined with a vertical cavity-forming damp proof course behind new plastering. External faces of existing stone walls were sandblasted to remove the layers of limewash and the stonework was then re-pointed with recessed joints in lime mortar.

It was a feature of old Anglesey stone external walls that they were built up of two revetments of rubble stone, one on the outer face of the wall and one on the inner face. The space between these two facings was then filled with earth and loose small stones, thus providing something of a primitive cavity wall in which some of the rainwater penetrating the outer skin could filter down through the loose filling to the foot of the wall and not all of the rainwater would thus find its way through to the inner face of the wall.

The house from the shore

A bedroom-wing extension was built to reflect exactly the revealed form of the original cottage, that new wing being placed at an obtuse angle to the existing structure to protect the sea front terrace from the south-westerly winds. Jim Greenwood, my loyal assistant for over 30 years (including a few of the years within the period covered by this book) is seen taking his ease in the photograph.

This is an appropriate place to list the names of other assistant architects who worked with me on the projects illustrated here, together with my note of appreciation for that involvement, whether on just a single house or further work over several years within this early, 'special houses for special people' period of the practice. I sign off this penultimate vignette therefore with a time-honoured thank you to Laurie Williams, Peggy Rogers, Keith Brettel, Richard Harris, Michael Longfield, Patrick Garnett, Michael O'Connor, Leonard Foinette and Ian Swallow for their parts in this saga.

Griff Roberts house

One of the consequences of having a one-principal architectural practice which concentrated, during the earlier years, on new private houses and domestic conversions, is that one gets to know a large number of families quite well. Very often, the initial commissioning meeting would take place at a family gathering over luncheon or afternoon tea and, thereafter, there would be several other similar meetings until such time as the design proposals had been agreed and work was about to commence on the building contract. It is of the nature of such meetings that family likes and dislikes, previous dwellings and other landmarks of family history will be revealed and discussed in relation to the requirements for the new house. Lasting acquaintanceships are established and many embryonic friendships emerge from these family encounters. House-warming parties at the completion and occupation of the finished dwelling are an enjoyable part of these relationships, often to be followed by reciprocal invitations for later prandial gatherings.

One of the earliest job numbers for my young office was that for Mr G I Roberts. Griff Roberts was an orthopaedic surgeon based at the Bangor hospitals and he lived at a turn-of-the-century house on the outskirts of the city. A second garage was required for the house together with alterations to the ground floor cloakroom arrangements. There were also some dry rot problems in joinery backing onto external walls. All these matters were dealt with during the following year, the only difference of opinion arising between us being the wish of Mr and Mrs Roberts to strip out some delightful solid oak panelling which lined the walls of the entrance hall, which I did my utmost to avoid. This is all some 50 years ago and I cannot now remember who won that particular argument!

A family friendship did indeed emerge from those early meetings with Griff and Jean Roberts and Dorothy and I saw them socially on many occasions over the next few years.

Over those years the desire of the Roberts to build their own new house across the waters of the Menai Straits in Anglesey was touched upon occasionally but, in the 1960s the desire intensified into an even more urgent search to identify the ideal site for the house. I accompanied them on many excursions in the area of Beaumaris, the preferred district, to look at possible sites, but the difficulty was always one of finding a generously-sized semi-rural site for which a planning permission for a single dwelling would be forthcoming. This period of the history of the new house for the Roberts therefore lasted for two or three years, with a growing feeling of despair that a suitable site would ever be found!

The frustrations of such single-house site searches were experienced with a number of clients during this period. The further away from the private house, non-building years of the 1940s we moved, the more difficult it became to find sites which had not been snapped up by others and the more severe became the planning authority restrictions in relation to the development of such sites.

When all hope for a site for the Roberts seemed to have evaporated I received a call one morning to say that they at last had in view just the site they wanted, albeit on the Menai Bridge side of Beaumaris rather than on the country side of that town. It did however, look to my client as though it might be too expensive to develop, being steeply sloped and rocky. Would I cast my eye over the site before a decision to purchase was taken? This I did and pronounced that a fine house could be built on this one-acre site more or less within the envisaged budget.

The house from the drive entrance

The drive arrives at the house

This house was not the last to be built within the 'special houses for special people' period reviewed here, although it was built close to the end of that period. I have however, left it until the last to be illustrated as, in many ways, it became probably my favourite one-off house of this period out of the more than 100 which were designed and built during these 15 or so years. (There are 80 named houses in this book, with another 20 or so which have not been illustrated and listed).

The problems posed by the steeply sloping site were resolved by building the house at the very top of the acre of gardens where the gradient eased off a little and by building a steep, hairpin drive up to the position of the house from the shore road below.

As can be seen from the photographs, from that position the house commanded wonderful views of the Straits and the Caernarfonshire shoreline beyond. Some of the terracing surrounding the southern corner of the house had to be cantilevered out over the rocky strata to take full advantage of the views and the sunshine during the early part of the day.

Affinity with the site and the fact that the house would be seen almost solely from well below, from the coast road or from the steeply sloping drive, led to a decision to keep a low profile for the house. It was also the case that, with Jean Roberts being a semi-invalid, it was necessary to site the master bedroom suite at ground floor level. There was thus plenty of room to accommodate the study bedrooms for the two children within the roof area, served by dormer windows, but without partly sloping ceilings interfering with the use of these first floor rooms. Local stone was used to relate the house to the rock outcrop on which it was built, Dinorwic slate was used for the roof and the rendered walls were coloured in contrasting areas of white and dark brown.

This was a happy contract. The Lingard/Roberts' family friendships continued for many years after the completion of this, perhaps my favourite, new house from these days of long ago.

SPECIAL HOUSES FOR SPECIAL PEOPLE

Photographic credits by chapter numbers

Numbers in brackets relate to the position of the photographs in a chapter. Where no number appears in brackets, all photographs in the chapter are by the named photographer.

Stewart Bale, Liverpool
1(1), 2, 4, 5, 6, 7, 8, 11, 13, 14, 19(1/4), 21(1), 24, 26(1/2), 27(2), 28, 30(1), 31(4), 33, 34, 36(1/2/3), 38, 39(2/4), 40, 41, 42, 46, 48(1), 49, 50, 54, 55, 60.

Emrys Jones, Colwyn Bay
16, 17, 19(2/3), 20, 21(2), 26(3), 27(1/3), 31(1/2/3), 32, 35, 39(1/3), 58.

Meyer, Oswestry
56(2), 59.

BHL
1(2/3), 3, 9, 10, 12(2), 15, 18, 22, 23, 25, 36(4), 37, 44, 45, 47, 48(2), 52, 53, 56(1).

SPECIAL HOUSES FOR SPECIAL PEOPLE

Bibliography

Chapter	Title	Author	Publisher	Date
1	The Welsh House	Iowerth Peate	Hugh Evans & Sons	1946
3	Portrait of an Architect	Raglan Squire	Colin Smythe	1984
5	The History of Architecture on the Comparative Method	Banister Fletcher	Batsford	1896 1st Ed.
7	The Modern House in England	FRS Yorke	Architectural Press	1944
7	New Houses for Moderate Means	Dalton Clifford	Country Life	1957
8	Across the Straits	Kyffin Williams	Duckworth	1973
11	Pioneers of Modern Design	Nikolaus Pevsner	Faber and Faber	1936
11	An Introduction to Modern Architecture	J M Richards	Penguin	1940
11	Oeuvre Complete	Le Corbusier	W. Boesigner	Various
15	The Good Food Guide	Raymond Postgate	Good Food Club	from 1951
18	My Brother Denys	Nicholas Monsarrat	Chariot Books	1948
22	Hugh Casson	José Manser	Viking	2000
23	Wild Wales	George Borrow	Murray	1862
25	England's Thousand Best Houses	Simon Jenkins	Allen Lane	2003
25	Llandudno's Alice Trail	I W Jones	Pegasus	1999
32	Good and Bad Manners in Architecture	Trystan Edwards	Allan	1924
35	Shorelands Summer Diary	C Tunnicliffe	Collins	1952
36	The Birds	Aristophanes		Circa 400BC
37	The Elements of Architecture	Henry Wotton		1642
37	De Architectura	Vitruvius		1st C BC
38	Rhosneigr Now and Then	T Hale	Hedgerow	1990
39	The Cruel Sea	Nicholas Monsarrat	Cassel	1951
47	Ancient Monuments in Angelsey	Royal Commission on Ancient and Historical Monuments in Wales		1937
49	They and I	Jerome K Jerome	Hurst and Blackett	1909
50	Madocks and the Wonder of Wales	E Beazley	Faber	1967
52	The Skeptical Environmentalist	Bjorn Lomberg	Cambridge Press	2001